The Real Faith for Healing

by

Dr. Charles S. Price

Bridge-Logos *Publishers*

North Brunswick, NJ

The Real Faith for Healing
by Charles S. Price
Previously published as *The Real Faith*
This new edition, completely revised and updated, 1997
International Standard Book Number: 0-88270-739-6
Library of Congress Catalog Card Number: 97-73698
Copyright © 1997 by **Bridge-Logos Publishers**

Published by:
Bridge-Logos *Publishers*
North Brunswick Corporate Center
1300 Airport Road, Suite E
North Brunswick, NJ 08902

Table of Contents

Introduction

Charles Price (1887-1947) was an orator par excellent. He was originally from Britain and trained in law at Wesley College, Oxford. Even before he was saved he could hold audiences spellbound with his great gift of communication. I once watched him move an audience of ministerial trainees to tears by merely reciting the alphabet three times, then on the fourth time he moved them to laughter. What was all the more remarkable is that he told us in advance what he was going to do. He then challenged us to recognize the difference between emotion and the anointing of the Holy Spirit when we entered the ministry.

Dr. Price had a conversion experience at a Free Methodist mission in Spokane, Washington, but was enticed into modernism. In the mercy of God, he attended Aimee Semple McPherson's meetings in my birthplace—San Jose, California—and was filled with the Holy Spirit. From that moment on he became a blazing flame of evangelism and a channel for divine healing wherever he went.

It was my privilege as a teenager to attend several camp meetings in Chehalis, Washington, where Dr. Price was the featured speaker. He usually stayed in the prayer room until time for the sermon. When he walked onto the platform, such a wave of divine glory accompanied him that the vast congregation of persons often stood to their feet shouting praises to the Lord for a protracted time.

I remember being spell-bound as he preached. He was a master communicator, but with that, he had a dynamic of the

Spirit that was overwhelming. Frequently we listeners would be so overwhelmed that we spontaneously stood to again praise the Lord. If this interruption was prolonged, as it so often was, Dr. Price would simply take a seat on the platform and wait until we calmed down. He would then resume his sermon as though nothing had happened.

At the end of his sermon, he offered to pray for the sick. This was not a phenomenon to me, for I was raised in a Pentecostal preacher's home. Praying for the sick was a normal part of our worship services. What amazed me was the tremendous authority Dr. Price had over sickness and demons. He did not suggest or plead. He commanded and it was done! Miracles happened right before our eyes.

He was a mighty evangelist who often had one thousand conversions per day in his campaigns. His pattern was to go into a community and stay until "the heavens opened." This often meant staying for weeks on end. I pastored a church in Eugene, Oregon, where many years before my arrival, Dr. Price preached in the Armory for weeks until they got "a break-through." That open window to heaven remained long after he left. I enjoyed the fruit of his labor years after he was dead.

His ministry predated the current popularity of Christian magazines. There were no tape recorders in his day, but he founded a small monthly teaching magazine he called *Golden Grain.* God greatly used his publication to touch persons who never saw or heard him, and many who did hear him subscribed to the publication to keep track of his campaigns and to be refreshed with his teaching. I still have a small shelf of these magazines in my library.

My most vivid memory of Dr. Price was when I was a student at Southern California Bible College. At that time the school was in Pasadena, California, not too far from Dr. Price's residence. Every Friday morning we students were privileged to have this great man of God for special lectures.

By this time he was retired and in failing health, but he spoke with such fervency and with such divine authority that we students were moved deeply. He pled for holiness of life, fervency of spirit, and integrity of behavior in each of us. He spoke of faith as though it were a commodity God imparted into a believer's life. I remember that his vocabulary was so much larger than mine that I would often fill a notebook page with words I did not understand. What sticks in my mind is the way he wove those words into his message. Although I may not have known the word, I didn't miss the meaning of the sentence.

Few men have more deeply challenged me to a life of faith. Every time I heard him, I wanted to be like him. Of course I did not succeed in this dream, but I am convinced that my life reached a higher plane in God because of what I saw and heard in Dr. Charles Price. He was a champion in the early Pentecostal movement.

He has, of course, gone to his reward, and earth is poorer because of this. Still, through the modern miracle of printed books, we can take a look backward at this man and see some of the principles and practices that made him such a valuable tool in the hands of our Master, Jesus Christ. What the Bible says of Abel can also be said of Dr. Charles Price, "He being dead yet speaketh" (Hebrews 11:4).

Judson Cornwall

Foreword

Dr. Charles S. Price had one of the most miraculous ministries ever seen. So miraculous, in fact, that some of the miracles truly staggered the imagination and stumbled the faith of many because they were so astounding. A few of them are recorded in the two sections in this rewritten and enlarged book.

This book was originally titled *The Real Faith*, and was self-published by Dr. Price in 1940. In 1972 it was published by Logos International. Since that time it has been through a multitude of reprints and has enabled thousands of readers to find the real faith they needed for help and healing.

Dr. Price died in 1947, so *The Real Faith* was not written in the early years of ministry, as so many books are today, but was written after nearly twenty years of ministry by a seasoned veteran of numerous battles of faith who could look back over the years with clarity and understanding. The miracles that Christ worked through Dr. Price were great and many, yet the heart of this man who knew Christ so well was constantly troubled by the suffering and disappointment of the many who weren't healed.

As the years of ministry grew, Dr. Price continually asked himself, "Why have our prayers so often gone unanswered? Why are our churches filled with the sick and dying who listen to sermons on divine healing that are true to the Word and promises of God, and yet are not healed when they're prayed for?" Finally, in the twilight years of his ministry, Dr. Price found the answer, and wrote this book to tell the answer to all who had eyes with which to read, ears with which to listen, and hearts with which to believe.

Why was this book rewritten? Dr. Price was a great orator, after the style of William Jennings Bryan. His sermons are filled with grand flourishes as he spoke of the wonders of God and Christ—and he wrote the same way. When his book was first published, it matched well his speaking style, and most of his readers were familiar with it. But as the years have passed, the art of oratory has virtually vanished, and books written in that style are increasingly difficult for modern readers to follow and understand. For that reason, we rewrote this book in the leaner and faster style that most readers today are accustomed to. In so doing, however, we were careful to retain and clarify all of Dr. Price's teaching on the real faith that so answered his questions, satisfied his heart, and brought help and healing to thousands.

In addition, we rewrote a section on miracles from his biography and added it to this book. It contains instructions on how to receive your healing, and how to maintain it. It also contains several testimonies of outstanding healings to encourage your faith.

Finally, we changed the title of the book from *The Real Faith* to *The Real Faith for Healing* to better identify the contents of the book. Within the book, we have further broken it down into two sections: *Section I, Real Faith; Section II, Healing.*

Knowing that Dr. Price's primary concern was to help the suffering to receive healing from the living Christ, we don't believe he would object that we have made changes in his material for that same reason.

Harold J. Chadwick, Editorial Director
Bridge-Logos Publishers

Section I

Real Faith

1

Something Was Wrong

For years I knew something was wrong. What it was I now know, for the Holy Spirit has shown me new beauty in that grace we call faith. I call it a grace because that's what it is. In our blindness we have taken faith out of the spiritual and put it into the metaphysical realm. Our emotions and desires have driven faith from the heart into the mind.

Why have our prayers so often gone unanswered? Why are our churches filled with the sick and dying who listen to sermons on divine healing that are true to the Word and promises of God, and yet are not healed when they're prayed for?

Often I've gone home from a meeting with shouts of victory ringing in my ears—but I've gone home to weep and cry before my Lord. The crowds were shouting because a few were healed, but I was weeping because of the many who dragged their tired, sick, bodies back to their homes—unhealed! I could not understand why some were healed in such a miraculous way, and others dismissed with an appeal to keep on believing and return later, only to go through the same formula again.

We must face facts. We cannot dismiss the discrepancy between theology and experience with a shrug of the shoulders, and refuse to ask for light and guidance on this all-important problem. Only the truth can make us free from the doubts and discouragement that ultimately come with our disappointments. The only way to learn the truth is to go in honesty of heart and mind to Jesus Christ, who said He Himself is the truth. So I am going to be painfully frank. I cannot spread my heart out over these pages and be otherwise, for never have I been so stirred as I am now. This glorious and wonderful truth has flooded my soul and lifted me in spirit to the gates of the glory world! I believe and pray that before you finish these chapters, you too will see the gates of grace swing open, and your feet will walk down the paths of faith to the place where you will meet your Savior in the garden of answered prayer.

I'm not a dogmatist and I don't wear robes of infallibility. I'm a grateful child of God to whom the Holy Spirit has given light about a subject that was viewed through a glass darkly in years past. But now, through the love of Christ, I have received at least partial understanding of the real and genuine faith of which Jesus not only spoke, but imparts to us.

The revelation has answered my questions. It has solved my problems. It has deepened my love for my Lord, and strengthened my surrender of heart and life to Him. It has revolutionized my healing ministry, for it has revealed to me the helplessness of self and the need of the presence, love, grace, and faith of Christ.

Through the years there have been thousands and thousands of miracles; and they prove beyond question that

Jesus is the "same yesterday, and today, and forever" (Hebrews 13:8). Not that we should rely upon experience to prove the Word, but it is blessed indeed when we can see manifestations of answered prayer. Yet how often I've gone home with the faces of poor supplicating people haunting me. I've seen them try to rise from their wheelchairs, only to drop back again in sorrow and disappointment. I've listened to their cries and prayers and the sound has lingered with me for days after the services were over.

You have also. In your church there are sick and needy people whose burdens seem to be too great for prayer. Ministers have told me of their discouragement because they could not exercise active faith in God. If it wasn't that once in awhile some suffering soul reached through and brought the glory down, many of these ministers would turn away when asked to pray for the sick. They're bewildered by what seems to be a contradiction between Word and experience.

It isn't right to sing, "Jesus never fails," and then have the sick leave with their burdens still with them. It's one thing to dismiss them with the words, "only believe," but it's another thing entirely to dismiss them from your thoughts and heart. To testify to healing on the basis of faith, before the healing has happened, is generally unwise and always inexcusable—unless *real faith* is actually there. Even when it is, it's far better to testify with the double witness of praise and thanksgiving and the manifestation of the healing.

Real faith that weighs no more than a mustard seed will do more than a ton of will and determination. For you can no more have real faith without result than the sun can shine without light. Now since real faith never fails to bring about the result, what is it that we have mistakenly called faith? Simply put, *we have failed to understand the difference between faith and belief.* To believe in healing is one thing; but to have faith for it is altogether something else. That's why so many needy people who believe come to the Lord on the basis of His

5

promises and try to *affirm* that they're healed—thinking that by so doing they *actually* will be healed.

Our Difficulty

Therein lies our difficulty. We have made faith a condition of the mind, when it is a divinely imparted grace of the heart. Beloved, we have been wrong in our attitude and practice. When the sunlight of God's grace and truth floods our hearts and minds, there will be an end to our struggling, and these hearts of ours will be wrapped in His garment of peace. In that hour we'll realize that *we can receive faith only as He gives it.* No longer will we struggle to believe. In the Galilee storm, the disciples could have worked themselves into a frenzy trying to still it's fury. But just three words from Jesus, "Peace, be still" (Mark 4:39), and the wind dropped from a scream to a whisper, and the sea grew quiet and still. Three little words from Jesus and the wind and sea obeyed Him. The storm would have laughed at the disciples though they spoke a million words of commands and rebukes in their determination to believe, for the storm knew it was greater than they were.

Three little words from Jesus—one touch from His hand divine—and more is accomplished in the time of a lightning flash than all our struggles and mental efforts could work in a thousand years. We have made it difficult, when He wanted to make it easy. My heart has cried as I have seen needy souls struggling so hard to exercise what they thought was faith—when in my heart I knew it did not come that way. At moments like that it was hard to say *anything*, for it meant the overthrow of established methods and doing away with certain actions that for years have been foolishly associated with the exercise of faith. It meant that having arrived at the end of honest effort without the thing for which we had prayed and tried to receive, we would have to conclude that there was something wrong in our attitude of soul and mind—or else victory would have been won.

In what way have we been wrong? I'm sure in my heart that I know the answer, that I've discovered what has been wrong. I can see now where so many missed the way. The only thing to do is to ask the Spirit to lead us back to the fork in the road where, because of our blindness, we left the path. Then once again we can walk on the King's highway of grace and prove in heart and experience that *the Word is true and Christ never fails.*

Remember that!

If there have been disappointments because of failures, the failures have been ours—not the failures of our Lord Jesus.

2

Till All Our Struggles Cease

One of the difficulties is our failure to see that faith can be received only as it is imparted to the heart by Christ. Either you have faith, or you do not. You can't manufacture it, and you can't work it up. You can believe a promise, and at the same time not have the faith to appropriate it. But we've tried to appropriate by belief, forgetting that belief is a mental quality, and that when we try to believe ourselves into an experience, we're getting into the metaphysical realm.

Real faith is spiritual, and warm and vital. It lives and throbs, and its power is irresistible when it's imparted to the heart by the Lord. "If thou . . . believe in thine heart that God hath raised him from the dead, thou shalt be saved" (Romans 10:9). Heart-belief opens the door of communication between us and the Lord and a divinely imparted faith becomes possible.

For most of us, our concept of faith has only resulted in our struggling to believe. Sometimes with all our struggling we came to the place where we did believe, and then we were bewildered by the fact that we didn't receive the thing we prayed for. So we must recognize that *such belief isn't necessarily what the Word calls faith.* In later chapters I'll give you many Scriptures that prove beyond question the truth of this alarming statement.

According to the Word of God, all we need is faith as a grain of mustard seed and the things the world calls impossible will be brought to pass. (See Matthew 17:20.) Many times I've seen Scripture stories come alive before my eyes as the Lord imparted His blessed faith, and the faith came almost every time without effort or struggle, as natural as the bright morning sun breaking over the horizon.

The seventeenth chapter of Matthew is a chapter of contrasts. It climbs into heaven and goes down into the valley. It talks of a mountain of transfiguration, a valley of despair, and a mustard seed—what a lesson the Holy Spirit has given us on this great subject of faith through its priceless Words. Down from the mountain of Transfiguration came our blessed Lord. Down from the gates of heaven itself, where robes of glory enclosed Him in God's own light. Down from a place of holy communion and encouragement to a place of defeat and despair, for at the foot of the mountain lay a valley of anxiety and bewilderment.

There was sickness there. A crushed and bleeding heart was there. A father crushed in spirit and heart was there. Preachers were there, too. They had gone through the faith formula. They had rebuked the devil. They had shouted and commanded and prayed just like we've done a hundred times, and yet the thing they prayed for did not happen. Even as with you and I.

Then Jesus Came and Spoke

With Jesus there was no struggle, no shouting, and no long and fierce battle to bring the answer to an anguished father's prayer. He spoke—the devil fled. A happy boy cuddled in his father's arms and sobbed his gratitude to God. A happy father embraced his boy and looked with tear-stained eyes of adoration at the face of the Man before whom devils flee.

Then again Jesus spoke. In answer to His disciples' question regarding their defeat, he said: "Because of your unbelief: for verily I say unto you, If ye have faith as a grain of mustard seed, ye shall say unto this mountain, 'Remove hence to yonder place;' and it shall remove; and nothing shall be impossible unto you." What a statement! All we need is faith as a grain of mustard seed and mountains will tremble as we approach.

Do you realize what Jesus said? *The least amount of faith that He could give was mightier than the largest amount of the devil's power.* Like the story of David and Goliath, a mustard seed went to battle against a mountain and slew it—but it required the faith that Christ alone can impart.

Did those disciples believe? Yes! They believed in Jesus. They believed His promises. They believed in divine healing, or they would never have held the healing meeting that day. Believing just like you and I have believed in healing services and in our church meetings, they prayed and commanded—but nothing happened. What they needed, according to Jesus, was faith—not a carload of it, but just a little faith—as a grain of mustard seed. That would be enough. That would be all that was necessary—if it was *real faith.*

When a woman in a meeting one night told me that she had all the faith in the world for her healing, I regretted to have to tell her that if I had faith as a grain of mustard seed—just that much of my Master's faith—greater miracles than we had seen would have been wrought in the mighty name of Jesus.

Isn't it evident that when we have prayed what we thought was the prayer of faith and nothing happened, it must be that what we thought was faith was not faith at all? Did Jesus say that "faith as a grain of mustard seed" would work sometimes and not at others? Read the text again. His declaration was plain and specific. There was nothing ambiguous about it. It was a clear statement of fact from the lips of the eternal God Himself— and who can speak with greater authority than He can?

Whenever and wherever this faith is active, we won't be standing around poor, sick folks hour after hour, rebuking, commanding, struggling, and pleading as in the past. There is a place for intercession, but it isn't when real faith is present. When Christ's faith is imparted, the storm dies down and there's peace in the soul. The only sound is the voice of thanksgiving and praise. That's when we realize that it wasn't our ability to believe that made the sickness go, but that Christ's faith was given. When we understand that, His glory will blaze though our souls like the first rays of morning sunlight that drive the night shadows away.

Then it will be morning, glorious morning in our souls! We can believe in the morning, we can love in the morning, we can have confidence in the morning, but only God can send the morning. Even so, we can believe in healing, we can believe in our blessed Redeemer and His power to heal, but only the Lord Jesus Christ can work the work that will lift us to the mountain peaks of victory.

The mistake with many is that they confuse Christ's imparted faith with their mental ability to believe. To sit down and repeat, "I am healed—I am healed—I am healed," is not only unscriptural but spiritually dangerous. I admit that such a spiritually unsound method might help a few neurotics, but it would never remove the mountain that the Master said faith would.

12

I remember a man in a wheelchair who was like hundreds of others that you and I have seen. Around him were grouped a dozen people who were doing everything in their power to get him out of that chair. There were prayers and tears mixed with commands and rebukes, and every sincere effort was tried to get him to walk. But though he tried time and again, he met only failure.

Later, when I talked with him quietly, he told me that he had been trying so hard to believe. He informed me that he once had lots of faith but now was bewildered and did not know what to do. I soon discovered that he had been entirely wrong as to what faith really is. *He thought he would be healed if only he could believe that he was healed.* That was what he was struggling and trying to do.

He believed God's promises. He believed Christ could heal him. He believed so many things—wonderful and glorious to believe in these days of doubt and fear—but he was trying to do the impossible. He was staking the working of the miracle on his ability to believe mentally that it was done.

I told him the story of a visit I once made to the house where Jesus turned the water into wine. I told him of how the Holy Spirit spoke to my heart as I stood before the water pots in that house. I asked him if he believed the Bible story of the miracle that the Master did in Cana of Galilee. He told me that he did. As my thoughts turned back to that afternoon in Cana, I again felt the warm glow of the presence of the Holy Spirit.

This is the lesson I received that day. Though the mother of Jesus and the disciples were there, would that water have turned into wine if they had merely believed that it was wine? No, of course not! It required the word of Jesus and the touch of God's hand. They could fill the pots with water, they could fill them to the brim, they could carry them to the appointed place. They could do the things He told them to do, for He never asks men to do the impossible. That power He reserves for Himself.

13

All things are possible with God. But Mark 9:23 tells us, "If thou canst believe, all things are possible to him that believeth." The belief that Jesus is speaking of here is not head belief or mental acquiescence, but the heart-belief that is real faith. This is proved by the story Matthew tells of the lunatic. In the account by Matthew, Jesus said, "If ye have faith as a grain of mustard seed"—while in the account by Mark it is, "If ye believe." So the "belief" of Mark and the "faith" of Matthew are identical. That's my point. That's what the Holy Spirit has made my poor eyes see. Faith is not intellectual, but spiritual! It is of the heart—not of the mind. Real faith is not our ability to "count it done," but is the deep consciousness divinely imparted to the heart that it is done. It is the faith that only Christ can give. "Looking unto Jesus the author and finisher of our faith" (Hebrews 12:2).

So I told my story to the man in the wheelchair. Did you ever see a flower open to the morning sun? I saw one that day as I looked into the face of that dear old man. Home he went to patiently wait until the Holy Spirit whispered in his soul that Jesus of Nazareth was passing by on the Jericho Road of his life.

A few nights later he came back in his wheelchair. I met him. "I'm going to walk tonight," he declared. His eyes were bright with faith.

"How do you know it?" I asked him.

"It's so quiet and peaceful in my soul," he said. "I'm so happy in the consciousness of His presence, that all I need now is to obey His word and be anointed in His blessed name." There was no struggle this time, not even intercession, for that had gone before.

There is no need for the twilight struggle between darkness and light after the rays of sunshine have kissed the earth—no place for the darkness when the sun comes up over the hill. Out of his wheelchair he got and walked the length of the altar—then down on his knees he went in adoration, praise, and worship, to pour out his grateful heart in thanksgiving for the heart-belief, or *real faith,* that comes only from God.

The Master's Visit

The mailman has just left a letter that I want to share with you. It's the story of a woman who was crippled beyond any I have seen in the many years I've presented my Lord as the savior of the soul and the healer of the body. When I first saw this woman, she begged piteously for prayer. She asked me to heal her. I could not, and I knew it. I might have gone through a series of commands, rebukes, and pleadings—but I did not. I was just a disciple at the foot of the mountain, and I knew that we both needed our Lord to come down.

I believed in Jesus and His power to raise the fallen. I believed His promise, and I stood on His Word. But as I looked into the face of a woman who had crawled on her hands for ten years, and who was helpless from the waist down, my heart told me that I needed more than just to believe she was healed. I needed the imparted faith that supersedes reason. I needed that spiritual quality of heart-belief that no mental affirmations of mind could ever bring about. I knew that was what she needed, too.

So I pleaded with her to contact Jesus. I begged her to wait patiently for the Lord. Her hour would come—I felt it in my heart. I knew that Jesus never fails. But how many times we prevent His working by our foolish efforts to do what He alone has power to accomplish. So day after day her husband and friends carried her to the meetings. Day after day she sought the face of the Lord. Night after night they picked up her helpless body and placed it before the old wooden bench where prayer was often made.

The days passed. In spirit she climbed the temple steps into the tabernacle of the Lord. She passed by the altars of surrender and sacrifice—and one night she entered into the

Holy of Holies, into the very presence of God. What a night! It was Sunday. Healing was not on the program that had been printed by human hands. But God works wonders when Jesus of Nazareth passes by—it is then that the Holy Spirit makes us rise above our forms, rituals, and plans.

A beautiful spirit pervaded that Sunday evening service. Down at the altar where she had been carried by her husband, the woman reclined to pray, for she could not kneel. Then Jesus came. He gave her a vision of Himself. She saw Him at the end of a road. He smiled. She was conscious of faith flowing like a river across her heart. Before it happened, she knew it! How, or why, she could not tell, but she knew that there had been a divine imparting of the faith of the Son of God.

At that very moment the Savior imparted His faith to my heart, too. I turned to the minister on the platform and said, "Tonight we shall see the glory of the Lord." We did.

As the hand of the Lord was laid upon the woman, she straightened out. Her shriveled limbs grew to normal size faster than it takes to tell it. She stood to her feet! She walked! No need to be carried now, except in the loving arms of Jesus.

Down to the foot of the Cross streamed sinners to seek a Savior! The building rang with the praises from joyous hearts, and the rafters resounded with the message:

> Only Jesus, only Jesus,
> Only He can satisfy.
> Every burden becomes a blessing,
> When I know my Lord is nigh.

Only Jesus

I told this story because I want you to see the difference between human effort to believe, and the faith that is the gift of God. How much better and more scriptural it is to wait until Jesus of Nazareth passes by and speaks the word of faith to the needy heart, than to mistake our belief in healing for the faith that He alone can give.

The day they first brought that poor, helpless, woman for prayer, I was aware of three things:

1. *She* did not have the faith *she* needed;

2. *I* did not have the faith *I* needed;

3. *Only Jesus* had the faith *we* needed.

So our mission was to draw close to Jesus. It's our privilege to take our troubles and cares to Him in prayer. Within our spiritual heritage is the right to draw apart from the world into the sacred place of communion, "where heaven comes down, our souls to greet, and glory crowns the Mercy-Seat." That's what we did. We could have set our minds and our wills to work right then and there. We could have commanded, exhorted, and entreated—and she could have struggled to rise, as others have done, in the power of will instead of in faith. But no, there's a better way. It's God's way. It's the Bible way. It was a long way for the nobleman to walk from Capernaum to Cana, but after he met Jesus he never regretted the journey. (See John 4:46-51.)

Now I want to share with you our sister's letter:

Laurel, Ontario
October 12, 1940

Dear Brother Price:
Christian greetings! Oh, hallelujah, the joy bells are ringing in my heart because of Jesus!

As the time draws near to another anniversary of the great miracle performed upon my body, the thoughts and the warmth of my husband's heart and mine go out to you in a very special way. Thank God, the blessed Christ came to us and manifested His power and presence so preciously to us, that evening, October 19, 1924.

What good measure He gave us! He saved my soul as well as healed my body, using you as His disciple. Truly I was in a pitiful condition, was I not, Brother Price? I was in great need both spiritually and physically.

Spiritually—I thought I was saved, but was really sort of on the fence, having too much of the Lord to enjoy the world, and too much of the world to have real joy in the Lord. Through your preaching the full gospel, the real joy of the Lord came into my heart, also my husband's, to abide—with the assurance that our many sins were washed away in Jesus' cleansing blood.

Physically—well, you pretty well know my condition in that respect, as you could see for yourself my helplessness when I was taken into your meetings, not being able to walk or stand, or even let my feet rest on the floor in the usual way when sitting in my chair. Ten long years of helplessness, being carried in the arms of my faithful husband, with continual suffering; and then, Jesus again walked the Jericho Road, and came my way in your meetings. Oh yes, you have heard me tell of it many times, but I want to tell it to you yet again. The story never becomes stale to my husband or me, because you see it is Jesus. Dear Jesus!

My heart overflows as I talk to you of it, and the tears are flowing too, for Jesus' love melts me down in praise and thankfulness before Him. Yes, Jesus heals sick bodies today! Keep on telling the good news, Brother Price, for there are so many sick and afflicted ones all about us. God's word tells us that Jesus healed the lame, the blind, the lepers, and all manner of diseases, when He walked this earth many years ago, and we do know that He does the very same in the days in which we live. His power has not lessened. Those bleeding, healing stripes He bore at Calvary are just as efficacious now as then, Thank God.

Sunday, October 19, 1924, Jesus put me upon my helpless feet and enabled me to walk without an ache or a pain; and sent me on my way rejoicing, and truly my husband and I have been rejoicing ever since—in Jesus! Sixteen years of health, strength and activity. I have had some real tests in my body during those years, broken bones and different trials of faith, but I want to tell you once again even though you so well know it, the promises of God hold fast and sure. Our God gets all the glory, for neither my husband nor I have ever used the slightest remedy of any kind since Jesus so undertook for us at Paris, where we found the great Healer in those gospel meetings.

In thankfulness and praise to Jesus, we again wish to thank you. Brother Price, for the part you had in the great work. Like Paul, you were not disobedient to the heavenly vision, for you did not compromise in any way, but declared the whole truth, not leaving out that Jesus heals the sick today.

My husband and I are so well in body, all glory and praise to Jesus our physician. Never any need for pills or liniment now; the promises are sufficient. Hallelujah! Jesus never, never fails.

We continue to pray for you. May you ever be guided by the Holy Spirit, and anointed from above for even greater service than in past years, to proclaim the unsearchable riches of Christ.

How the Holy Spirit warms me as I write, and the power of God thrills and fills me. Hallelujah! Jesus lives! How do we know? Thank God, because He lives within.

Cordial Christian love to you all, from your ever thankful friends in Jesus.

Brother and Sister Johnson

3

The Better Road

There is a difference between the faith of the Old Testament under law and the faith of the New Testament under grace. The key word of the epistle to the Hebrews is "better." The writer is showing them the truth of Christianity by using contrast. He doesn't do away with the past, but shows them that Christianity grew out of Judaism just as the flower grows out of the root.

Hidden away in the ritual of the root was the color, the fragrance, and the beauty of the flower of grace that was to come later. Was not the flower better than the root? Was not the end better than the beginning? Was not the blood of Christ better than the blood of the lambs? Was not Jesus better than the angels who had visited their fathers? Was not the voice of God's Son better than the voice of the prophets?

This is the heartthrob of the Epistle. When the author writes the faith chapter is there any reason he would depart from the purpose and motive of his letter? Of course not. The theme is still "better," and the purpose is to show the better faith of Jesus in comparison to those works and words of the patriarchs and prophets that were counted unto them as faith. Notice that the faith chapter closes with the words, "God having provided some better thing for us, that they without us should not be made perfect" (Hebrews 11:40).

In other words, the acts and testimonies of the ancients were held up like pictures in a gallery for the Christian Jews to behold and admire. There was the story of Abel, Enoch, Noah, Abraham, Sarah, Isaac, and Jacob, all framed as pictures of obedience to the divine word. Then there came Moses and Joshua, followed by a grand parade of the illustrious of the days before Jesus was born. But nowhere in the epistle does the writer tell us that our faith today should be limited to the pattern and operation of the faith of the Old Testament believers. He tells of something better. He introduces us to the flower that grew out of the root.

Faith in the old days was manifested by word and deed in obedience to command. But there is more. The word and deed are only a small part of what the New Testament teaches us that faith really is. Of course there is work and testimony, but those alone are not faith—not *New Testament faith.*

If you look in the Old Testament at the accounts of the men and women in the eleventh chapter of Hebrews, you'll see that the word *faith* is never mentioned in connection with their lives. The word *faith* is used in the Old Testament only twice—once prophetic, and once about the unbelief of a wicked generation. (See Habakkuk 2:4 and Deuteronomy 32:20.)

So the writer of Hebrews is not holding up the lives of these Old Testament believers as a pattern for the New Testament believers to follow, but rather as the beginning of something more wonderful that they were to discover in Jesus. The faith they were to possess was all the Old Testaments believers had and more. Seeing that they were surrounded by such a great cloud of Old Testament witnesses, they too were to lay aside weights and sins and run with patience the *new* race that was set before them. To do that, they were to look to Jesus who was the author and finisher of their faith. (See Hebrews 12:2.) If He was the author and the finisher of their faith, and the faith of the Apostles, then He is the author and finisher of our faith, too. All true faith begins and ends in Him. The verse doesn't say He's the author and the finisher of His faith, it says He's the author and finisher of *my* faith—and *yours!*

Faith and Presumption

There is nothing before the Alpha and nothing after the Omega. (See Revelation 1:8, 11.) He begins it, and it begins in Him. He ends it, and it ends in Him. When I want faith, I must seek Him. I can't get it anywhere but from that matchless One of whom it is said, He is "the author and the finisher of our faith."

After looking at the eleventh chapter of Hebrews and seeing what they did, have we then made the mistake of rolling up our sleeves to work and prove our faith by what we do? Have you ever done that? If you have, then you've stood in bewilderment at what seemed to be unanswered prayer and the inoperative power of what you thought was faith.

Remember this:

Faith acts—but the act comes from faith, and not faith from the act.

That's why it's easy to cross the line between imparted faith and presumption. Some years ago in Victoria, B. C., I was entering the Metropolitan Methodist Church with a few ministers when we saw an elderly lady being taken out of a truck in a wheelchair that was too large for a car. I raised my hat and said, "God bless you."

Her eyes misted as she replied, "He has been blessing me, Dr. Price. He is so kind and gracious, and I can feel His presence now."

"Have you come for healing?" I inquired.

"Yes, I have," she replied, "and praise His name, I know the waters are troubled."

Just then the truck driver leaned over and said, "Shall I come back, lady, to take you home after the service?"

A light came over her face and she replied, "No, I'm not going to need a truck. I'll leave my wheelchair behind and go home on the train." The driver scratched his head and grinned at her—probably thinking she was a foolish woman. Away he drove. And she did not need him! She went home healed and rejoicing—and she went on the train!

I told that story in a meeting I conducted in the middle west. The next day a lady sent a message that she would like to see me in her cottage. She was lying on a couch surrounded by a group of people singing a hymn. She said, "Brother Price, I have sent the wheelchair home." She waited for a shout from me. None came. Instead my heart fell. There was no faith and I knew it.

When she saw I did not enthuse over her act, she turned away and said, "If God can do it for one woman, He can do it for another."

Late that evening when I left the main building, she was again the center of a group who were insisting that she arise and walk, but she went away sorrowful. Of her the Lord could say, "There is one thing thou lackest." The two acts were the same. Two wheelchairs were sent home. In one case it was faith, and in the other it was presumption. In New Testament faith, *the act can be born of faith, but faith cannot be born of the act. The act can come from faith, but the faith must come from God.*

This, then, is the better way of the epistle to the Hebrews. This is the purpose and the motive back of what is called the 'faith chapter.' Have you a need or problem? Take it to Jesus. Lay it at the Master's feet. As you give Him your confidence and trust, you will find His faith will become operative in you. Why play with the teacup of our struggles and endeavors when His faith is vaster than ten-thousand ocean?

Christ is no respecter of persons. He loves the weakest and the simplest of us. But we become so important in our own eyes and so proud of our spiritual accomplishments that our testimonies display only the vanity of self- righteousness. We need to go to Christ as little children with guileless love overflowing our hearts. "Except . . . ye become as little children, ye shall not enter into the Kingdom of Heaven."

Steal away softly to Jesus. In this day of grace, the faith for the Christian can be found only in Christ; but in our blessed Lord you will find a sufficient supply for all your need. What Noah had was good, but what we have is better. Noah had God's Word, but we have God's Son. Noah built on God's Word, but our foundation is Christ Himself. The remarkable eleventh chapter of Hebrews is a recitation of God's glory manifest in the acts of those who believed God and walked in obedience with Him. Enoch went for a walk with Him one day and forgot to come back. When the faith that is of God came to earth in the Son of God, the writer to the Hebrews said, in effect, "That was the old faith, but here is the new. That was the good way, but this is the better."

A Story of Mueller

Christ was to be all in all. And the love of the Father's heart is shown in the fact that He is not only able, but willing to meet our every need. I have been reading the life of George Mueller, that great man of faith who raised millions of dollars to care for orphans and to support missionaries all around the world, without ever asking for money or indicating to anyone that he had need of it. Pastor Charles Parsons tells of a conversation he had with Mueller:

> A warm summer day found me slowly walking up the shady groves of Ashley Hill, Bristol. At the top there met my gaze the immense buildings which shelter over two thousand orphans, built by a man who has given the world the most striking object lesson in faith it has ever seen.
>
> The first house is on the right, and here, among his own people, in plain, unpretentious apartments, lives a saintly patriarch, George Mueller. Passing through the lodge gate, I paused a moment to look at House No. 3 before me, only one of the five erected at a cost of $600,000.
>
> The bell is answered by an orphan, who conducts me up a lofty stone staircase, and into one of the private rooms of the venerable founder. Mr. Mueller has attained the remarkable age of ninety-two. As I stand in his presence, veneration fills my mind. "Thou shalt rise up before the hoary head, and honor the face of the old man" (Leviticus 19:32).
>
> He received me with a cordial handshake, and bade me welcome. It is something to see a man by whom God has accomplished a mighty work; it is more to hear the tones of his voice; far more than either to be brought into immediate contact with his spirit, and feel the warm breath of his soul breathed into one's own. The communion of that hour will be forever graven on my memory.
>
> "I have read your life, Mr. Mueller, and noticed how greatly, at times, your faith has been tried. Is it with you now as formerly?" Most of the time he leaned forward, his gaze directed on the floor. But now he sat erect and looked for several moments in my face, with an earnestness that seemed to penetrate my very soul.

There was a grandeur and majesty about those undimmed eyes, so accustomed to spiritual visions and to looking into the deep things of God. I do not know whether the question seemed a sordid one, or whether it touched a lingering remnant of the old self to which he alludes in his discourses. Anyhow, there was no shadow of doubt that it roused his whole being. After a brief pause, during which his face was a sermon, and the depths of his clear eyes flashed fire, he unbuttoned his coat, and drew from his pocket an old-fashioned purse, with rings in the middle, separating the character of the coins. He placed it in my hands, saying: "All I am possessed of is in that purse, every penny! Save for myself ? Never! When money is sent to me for my own use, I pass it on to God. As much as £1,000 has thus been sent at one time; but I do not regard these gifts as belonging to me; they belong to Him, whose I am, and whom I serve. Save for myself? I dare not; it would dishonor my loving, gracious, all bountiful Father.

"The great point is never to give up until the answer comes. I have been praying for fifty-two years, every day, for two men, sons of a friend of my youth. They are not converted yet, but will be! How can it be otherwise? There is the unchanging promise of Jehovah, and on that I rest. The great fault of the children of God is that they do not continue in prayer; they do not persevere. If they desire anything for God's glory, they should pray until they get it. Oh, how good, kind, gracious and condescending is the One with whom we have to do! He has given me, unworthy as I am, immeasurably above all I had asked or thought. I am only a poor frail, sinful man; but He has heard my prayers tens of thousands of times, and used me as the means of bringing tens of thousands into the way of truth. I say tens of thousands in this and other lands. These unworthy lips have proclaimed salvation to great multitudes, and very many have believed unto eternal life."

Thus spoke George Mueller. Thus spoke a man of our times, for I was in Bristol as a boy while Mueller was yet alive. Thus spoke a man who had learned the lesson that waters come from the fountain and that flowers come from the root. He had learned that *the faith of God comes only from God* and that nowhere else could it be found. He learned that He who was so free in the grace of giving would teach His disciples how to be efficient in the grace of receiving. When Mueller needed money, he went not to the man who had it, but to the Christ who had the power to speak to the heart of the man who had it. His faith came because of his daily, vital contact with his Lord; and being in the will of God, he was given more than enough for every need.

Men used to call him "the nineteenth century apostle of faith." I suppose he must have heard that said about himself. I wonder if when he read the eleventh chapter of Hebrews, if he ever became conscious of the fact that men were adding his name to the roll of the heroes of faith. If he did, I think he must have smiled when he came to the last verse of that eleventh chapter of Hebrews and read, "God having provided something better for us." And he must have found what that better was when only two short Scripture verses away he found the words, "Looking unto Jesus, the author and finisher of our faith" (Hebrews 12:2).

So go to Jesus now. Learn to trust Him, that He might impart *His faith.* Acquaint Him with your need. Tell Him of your sorrows. Then, in the sanctuary of His presence, you will find rest and freedom from the noise and worries that beset you from without and within.

4

The Origins of Faith

I have a very decided dislike for negative preaching and writing. It's not sufficient for a speaker or author to discuss the disease, but to satisfy my soul and mind, he must give me the cure. It's easy to point out what is wrong, but I want to know what is right. Sometimes that's a little more difficult than one would suppose. However, when at last honest mistakes have been rectified, and we're back on the paths of truth, it may be that in the providence of God the wrong trail will have left us a heritage of blessing. For a long time we've been looking for faith on the wrong trail, so let us now get on the right trail that will lead us to *real faith.*

The thing above all else I want you to see is that you cannot generate faith, you cannot work it up, and you cannot manufacture it. *God Himself must impart it.* You cannot obtain faith by struggling or by affirming that something is, nor can you turn your hope and desire into faith by your own power. You can get faith only from the Lord, for the Word clearly states that faith is one of two things—a gift of God, or a fruit of the Spirit.

Paul wrote to the Corinthians, "Now abideth faith, hope, and love; but the greatest of these is love." While love might be the greatest, it certainly is not the first. It must be preceded by faith. Look at the wonder of a tree. What a thing of symmetry and loveliness it is. Only God can make a tree. There is beauty in its twisted branches. There is loveliness in its trembling leaves. Every leaf is a little world unto itself, with its tiny veins carrying the life that God supplies, which gives it all it possesses in its native realm. Yet there is something back of the tree. Beneath the surface of the ground there is a great system of roots hidden away. You never see them, yet without the roots the tree would die. It would have no life at all.

Faith is the Life

Tree roots are ugly and hard in comparison to the beautiful greenery above the ground. Yet the greenery is there partly because of those roots. Now, let's call the top of the tree "Love." You can see it, you can contact it, you can enjoy its fragrance. You behold its beauty. It's there because of something that is back of it, something hidden away that causes it. That something is the roots. Now is faith the roots? No. Faith is the *life* that flows into the roots—that spiritual quality that only God can produce and give—and the roots are your soul and spirit. It's essential that we understand what *real faith* is. The roots of the tree are not faith. *The roots do not produce the life, the life produces the roots.* It is the life that is faith— that wonderful and glorious quality that is a gift of the divine heart, and that sustains us. It would be foolish for a tree to struggle in an attempt to create the life that flows into it. It need not struggle. All it needs to do is function in obedience to divine laws and receive the life into itself. As the life flows into and through it, the tree simply manifests that life by the fruit it produces.

So it is with faith. Love may be the greatest thing in the world, but faith is necessarily the first. Without faith it is impossible to please God. Now if you tell me that you have faith, I will ask you where you got it. I pick a rosy apple from a tree. I hear it testify from the core of its apple heart. It tells me it has rosy cheeks. It whispers in my ear that it is good to the taste and good for me. It invites me to taste its flavor. It testifies that it has many noble and beautiful qualities. Then I ask it where it got them all.

From the branch? The shelter of the leaves, the rain, and the sun? All true. But to produce the fruit, I know that in the trees hidden parts beneath the ground, the roots received something from God that no tree on the face of the earth has ever been able to produce of itself. That something is *life*—that quality of life that makes trees grow and produce fruit.

The Atheist and God

Some time ago an atheist sat in a meeting I was conducting. He was hard and cynical. He lived alone in a hotel room, and his solitude had only added to his unbelieving nature. I preached that night on "Comprehending the Incomprehensible." I declared it was possible to believe the unbelievable, and to know the love of God that passes knowledge. The next day he came to my room and asked for an interview. He was argumentative, and I told him I did not have time for argument, but I would gladly answer any honest question that he had.

He said, "I have no faith whatever. I don't believe the Bible, and I don't know if there is a God. I do see a law of order in nature and the universe, but what causes it, or where it came from, I don't know. Now, Dr. Price, your sermon last night was a challenge to my thinking. What I want to know is this: How can a man spend a dollar when he doesn't have one? How can you drive a car when you don't possess one? How can you believe when you have no belief? How can God expect a man to exercise faith when he doesn't have any—assuming there is a God? Where is there any justice in a set-up like that?"

"Are you an honest man, and do you want to know the truth?"

"What is truth?" was the reply. "What kind do you mean? Whatever it is, I've never been able to find it."

I walked over to one wall of my room and stared at a picture of Jesus in the Garden of Gethsemane. You've seen the picture—Jesus is kneeling at a rock with his hands clasped and His eyes raised toward heaven. I knew that by so doing the man's eyes would be drawn to the picture. After a few moments, I turned to him and said, "Jesus is truth. Jesus is the way. Jesus is your life and faith. He has in abundance what you say you don't have—what you've been trying to get with your mind and intellect. He can put it there as a river of grace flowing through your heart. That's why He came. He came to make men free—free from doubts like yours, free from fears and misgivings, free from unbelief, free from sin, free from ... "

"Sounds like a fairy story to me," he interrupted. "Fine if you can believe it, but how can man or God expect a man to believe what he can't believe?"

He went away. A week later he came back. When I looked at his face, I knew the miracle had taken place and God had revealed Christ to his soul. "Do you know what happened?" he said. "I told the Lord to manifest Himself, if He was there. I asked Him to do something that would reveal His presence, if He was there at all. Then I became conscious that He was near me. I realized there was a God, and there was a soul to save—my soul. I didn't understand it with my mind, but I knew it in my heart. Then I told Him I had no faith to believe, so *He gave me His faith*, and I believed. The work was done."

Sound too simple to be true? It's not—that's God's way of salvation. "But as many as received Him, to them gave He power to become the Sons of God, even to them that believe on His name" (John 1:12). When I give an altar call, I invite *every* man, woman, and child to surrender their hearts and lives to Christ. Now, if we're saved by faith, how do I know that *all* can have the faith to receive? How do I know that everyone whom I invite can find eternal life? Some might have faith, and some might not. The fact that people *believe what you say* doesn't mean they have the faith to translate that belief—or desire—into experimental knowledge of sins forgiven.

Nevertheless, I cry "Whosoever will may come," because I know that *Christ will impart saving faith* to every *sincere* soul. The verse I quoted from John says, "But as many as received Him, to them gave He power to become the Sons of God, even to them that believe on His name," and the one after that completes the thought: "Which were born [that is, born again] not of blood, nor of the will of the flesh, nor of the will of man, but of God."

The Holy Spirit who gives the sinner enough conviction to convict him of his sin, will also give him enough faith to convince him of his salvation. No man in himself, however, possesses that faith—it *must* be given. Are we not told, "For by grace are ye saved, through faith; and that not of yourselves: it is the gift of God" (Ephesians 2:8). Unbelieving humanity, in the power of darkness, "having no hope, and without God in the world (Ephesians 1:12), could never develop in their sinful hearts enough faith to believe in Christ as savior, let alone receive Him. So the Holy Spirit *must* not only impart conviction of their need of a savior, but also impart the faith to receive Him.

Never think it was your faith that enabled you to receive Christ as your savior! Never say that any act of yours was the basis of your redemption. It is Jesus who imparts living water into your innermost being. It is Jesus who puts His arms of love beneath the burden on your back and lifts it from your weary body. It is Jesus who pours into your broken heart the oil of heaven's joy. It is Jesus who smooths your wrinkles of care with His gentle touch, and it is Jesus who brings you out of the power of darkness into the light of His glorious kingdom.

> Oh, it is Jesus; yes, it is Jesus;
> Yes, it is Jesus in my soul;
> For I have touched the hem of His garment,
> And His blood has made me whole!"

Sing it, shout it, proclaim it: His blood—His grace—His power—His pardon—*His faith!*

A Living Faith

When will we stop our foolish and needless struggles and begin to believe? When will we put an end to our unscriptural mental gyrations in our attempt to activate a faith we don't possess—for unless God gives us faith, we never will possess the faith we need for salvation or healing or anything else. *We are capable of belief and at the same time absolutely incapable of the exercise of Bible faith.* Thousands have wandered into the error of thinking that belief is faith. It is not. There is belief in faith, without a doubt, but "the devils also believe" (James 2:19). Belief is cold, intellectual, and operates only in the mind. Many sinful men believe the Bible, but such belief doesn't save them. Millions of Christians believe in healing, but such belief doesn't heal them.

Faith is living and irresistible. It moves with dynamic force and overcomes all doubt and unbelief and every enemy of the soul. All the faith in the world? No! You need only as much as a grain of mustard seed—*if it is God's faith!* Then mountains will be removed, and your sin-sick soul will behold the glory of the Lord. But it must be God's faith. It must come from Him. He must impart it. And He will. That is the Gospel of Grace that I believe.

The Jericho Road without Jesus is just a dry and dusty road. With Him, it's a shining highway of grace. Without Him, its dust is sordid, its tears are real, and its way is dark. But with Him, its dust turns to flowers of glory, its tears turn to pearls, and its darkness turns to light. But—*it takes the presence of Jesus to transform a Jericho Road into a highway of healing.*

Blind Bartimaeus did not sit in the sand and say to himself, "I am healed—I am healed—now if only I can believe I am healed, then I will be!" No. He heard that Jesus of Nazareth was passing by, and He cried, "Jesus! Jesus! Help me! Please help me, for I cannot help myself!" And Jesus asked, "What wilt thou that I should do unto thee?" Mark you, Jesus didn't tell him what *he* had to do, He asked him, "What do *you* want *Me* to do?"

True, He said, Go thy way; thy faith hath made thee whole." But where did Bartimaeus get the faith that healed him? If it was his faith, why wasn't he healed *before* Jesus came that way? If you give me a watch, it is my watch. But I got it from you. There's faith in my heart as I write, but I know where I got it. Not from affirmation—not from will—not from belief—not from mental exercises—I got it from Jesus. *He is the author and finisher of our faith!* My friend, if you'll learn to go to Jesus for the faith you need, the power of faith can be manifested in your life until men and angels will wonder. However, when the battle is over and the victory won, don't say, "Look at what I've done by my faith." Instead, kneel at the foot of the Cross and say, "Isn't it wonderful that by grace my Lord's faith was manifested through me."

5

Strength for Your Labor

I've written this book because it's my heart desire to show you the necessity of trusting in Jesus for *all* the needs of your life. Sometimes Christians must be brought down so they can learn to look up and see their true position in the grace of God. Self-righteousness is often born of continued victories. Because we overcome and are sustained by God's power and grace, we often develop the feeling that in ourselves we've become impregnable. Soon pride and self-righteousness begin to rear their ugly heads. We become so sure of ourselves and our position that we become a danger to ourselves. "Let him that thinketh he standeth take heed lest he fall" (1 Corinthians 10:12).

Christ has placed at our disposal resources of strength that only He can provide. It's recognition of the necessity of intimate contact with Christ—and the limitless possibilities that the contact brings—that means victory over sin and self as we travel toward heaven. Lose that contact and you lose both the hope and the possibility of a victorious life. *You are dependent upon Jesus for everything*, and He freely gives everything that you depend upon Him for. Whether or not you avail yourself of all He has for you, is dependent upon whether or not you've learned the lesson of drawing on His strength.

Read about this stupendous revelation in God's dealings with Abraham, the father of faith. Genesis 17:1 has a statement so powerful and beautiful that men must stand in awe and angels wonder. God was testing Abraham's faith. He had promised the ancient patriarch that from his loins would come descendants as numberless as the stars—that a great nation would arise from him, and all the families of the earth would be blessed because of his seed.

For hundreds of nights the old man dreamed of the happy day when that promise would be fulfilled. Many years passed— long, slow, years—and still the promised son did not come. Far too soon he was ninety, then ninety-five, and still he and Sarai waited in vain. Now he was ninety-nine and there was no son. Reason whispered fearful things in his ear. The ground seemed to tremble under his aged feet. His faith began to slip. Up to now his walk had been perfect—not in himself—but in his Lord. Misery and doubt became his companions. Reason whispered, "You fool, you're having a son is impossible." He thought of Sarai's age, she was almost ninety—and he was far past the age to produce children. How could it ever be? And yet—and yet—*there was God's promise*! Long and fierce raged the battle in the old man's heart and mind. He would not doubt—God Himself had promised!

El-Shaddai

One night a familiar voice spoke in Abraham's heart. His heart pounded and almost failed as he heard the awesome words of the voice that had spoken to him years before: "I am the Almighty God; walk before me, and be thou perfect." In Hebrew, "Almighty God" is "El Shaddai" What does it mean?

Basically, the word *El* means God and *Shaddai* means Almighty. El Shaddai is the name of God that sets Him forth primarily as the strengthener and satisfier of His people. Abraham might be weak, but God was strong. Men might be moved by the power of circumstance and the wicked forces of life, but God never. He is the Strong One. But what good does that do us? Suppose God is strong while we are so weak? To sit in our weakness, misery, and failure, and look at His strength only aggravates our lost condition. God is strong—no doubt about that—but what about our poor weakness and need? So it was with Abraham until God spoke to him and said, "I am El-Shaddai."

The word *Shad* is the Hebrew for "breast." It is used invariably throughout the Old Testament for the breast of a woman. It is the place from which the baby derives the food that gives it strength. The life of the mother flows into the babe. Her strength, love, solicitude, and care all flow into the life and body of the sweet little bundle that came from her and is always a part of her. Thus an eternal God wrapped up an infinite truth in picturesque words and gave it as a gift to Abraham—and to you and me.

What God meant was "Draw from Me, Abraham, all the strength and sustenance you need. I am the Strong One, the Nourisher, and the Life-Giver. Draw for your weakness from the fountain of my strength, even as a babe draws from his mother's breast the milk of life. No need to stumble over unbelief, Abraham, just walk before me and be perfect. That's the lesson. God is the unfailing and unlimited source of all that we need: grace to cover all our sins, love that pardons all our iniquity, stripes sufficient for all our healing, strength for all our weakness.

We believe that, but herein we've failed. We believe that God gives it, but we haven't learned how to receive it. The mother gives the milk to her babe, but the little one must receive it. The infusion of the divine strength and nature is dependent upon two things: your knowledge that God is willing to give, and your learning how to receive. As unfailing and irrevocable as the law of the seedtime and the harvest is the great truth that God is always ready to meet your every need, if only you are ready to receive His supply.

Praise His Name, He is still El-Shaddai! Paul admonished us to become "partakers of the divine nature," and Christ Himself said, "My grace is sufficient for thee." The God who was mighty enough and sufficient for every need of Abraham, longs for us to learn the lesson of drawing from Him all that we need for every moment of every passing day.

Who?

Elijah sat in defeat and spiritual disgrace. He had quit. He of the lion heart had been beaten on the battlefield of the soul by Ahab's wife, and that after he had faced an army! Then something happened. He went for forty days and nights without food unto Horeb, the mount of God. In whose strength did he go? Who strengthened David's heart and arm so he could defeat the giant Goliath? Who flattened the walls of Jericho? Who was with Joseph from the pit to the throne? Who delivered Israel from Egypt? Who led them into the Promised Land? Who opened the prison doors for Peter? Who gave Stephen grace to die and pray for his murderers? Who dried the tears of Martha and poured oil into the broken heart of Mary?

Who was it who saved our guilty souls, when we knelt at the foot of the Cross? Who turned our darkness into day? Who stands by our sides at this moment, ready and willing to give grace and glory? Who has strength for our weakness—

healing for our sickness—power for our trials—freedom for our slavery—and grace sufficient for every need? Who can it be, but Jesus Christ!

El-Shaddai still speaks to our hearts and, of a truth, we can still sing, "Strength for thy labor the Lord will provide." Draw upon His life. Take the grace He so freely and gladly imparts. He's more than sufficient for your need, and it's possible to walk before Him and be perfect, not in self, but in Christ. I know whereof I speak.

It's been my privilege to be called by my Lord to preach His gospel over the earth. The greatest joy of my life is to win souls, as He leads me and gives me strength for the task. Many of the campaigns ran from eight to ten weeks, and sometimes the body got very weary. One night I was sitting in an office in a corner of the tabernacle, feeling tired and at the end of my endurance. Out in the auditorium a great crowd was waiting for the service to begin, and through the thin boards I could hear the murmur of people at prayer. Then the door opened. A minister stood there and said, "Brother Price, there are about five hundred people here tonight who expect to be anointed in the name of the Lord for healing."

Five hundred—and I did not have the strength I needed to preach. Then there was that multitude to meet in the name of my Lord. In my heart I felt for a moment like running away. Then I wondered if I could dismiss the sick and tell them to come back some other night. I looked through a crack in the wall, and there I saw the poor sufferers waiting for an inadequate human like me to tell them of Jesus. Suddenly my nerves seemed to go to pieces. I dropped to my knees on the floor and wept. "Oh, Jesus," I cried, "I can't. I haven't the strength. I'm so weary and tired. I want to, Lord, but I'm not equal to this task."

Then I heard that still, small, voice in the depths of my heart. "You have no strength . . . Why not take mine?" For a moment I thought, *could this be real?* Why not? Did not the Lord give His strength to people in the olden days? Why not now. "Thank you, Lord," I said as I waited for what He would do. Then I felt a warm glow come over this body of mine. I walked out on the platform. Many times I preached from notes, but not that night. There was no weariness, no fatigue; nothing but the conscious knowledge of His strength.

In faith I assured the sufferers that all would be reached that night. When the midnight hour came, I was still laying these unworthy hands of mine upon human heads, in the name of the Lord Jesus. The power of the Lord was present to heal them, because the Lord Himself was there. Then it was over and I went home. As I was about to retire, I became conscious again of a great weariness. But I was not too tired to drop on my knees and thank Him for what He had done that night. He was still El-Shaddai. I knew that He had imparted His strength to meet my weakness. He will meet your weakness too. He will meet your every need, and no good thing will He withhold from them that walk uprightly.

One great requisite for the reception of the strength that He can give is that you feel your need of that strength. Our trust in Him is personal confidence, and when we come on the basis of His merit, He gives us His faith. We don't look *at* Jesus, but *unto* Him. So many follow Him afar off. They look at Him, but are not near enough to look unto Him. They lag behind while they dissect creeds, handle dogmas, contend with others about interpretations, and lose thereby the sweetness of His presence.

Which would you be?

Have you learned the lesson of drawing on Jesus for the needs of your life? Have you found the sweetness of abiding in the Lord? Have you come to the realization that after all is

42

said you're a miserable failure? Have you come to the place of the consciousness of your great need, and your pitiful lack of strength with which to overcome? Would you not rather be in the shoes of the publican on the temple steps than in the shoes worn by the Pharisee who felt so strong in his righteousness and so proud of his deeds? *Only as we decrease can Christ increase.* That means to decrease in our self-life, self-esteem, and self-confidence.

Christ can be your all in all, not only in doctrine, but also in practice and reality every moment in every day of the passing years. He invites you to prove Him. He admonishes you to test Him. Why be empty when you can be full to overflowing? Why be hungry when you can be fed? Why wander like a lost child on the desert wastes of life, crying because you know not the way of your tomorrows? Better by far to put your hand in His and hear the whisper of His voice divine, "Follow me; I'll guide thee home."

Then the things only dreamed of become real in Christ. The desert turns into a trail of flowers, the storm stills to a gentle whisper, and the trusting heart hears the music of heaven that no mortal ears can hear. The rocky hills are but the paths that lead upward to a transfiguration meeting place with El Shaddai, who has all authority and power in heaven and on earth.

At a camp meeting an elderly lady listened to the truth set forth on this printed page. She was so very sick! Over and over again she had been anointed; over and over again to no avail. At the end of the service I saw her sitting quietly, but the expression on her face told me of the conflict within. Suddenly she clasped her hands in prayer and said so appealingly, "Oh Jesus, I have tried so long with this poor faith of mine. Please give me some of Yours." He did! In a moment's time her sickness was scattered by the healing breath of God.

That's the secret of Christian victory. That's the secret of overcoming. Laying your burdens at His feet—to leave them there and never again carry them around like an old worn-out garment. That's the message of the "God Who is enough." Enough for whom? Why, for you, of course. Enough for when? For now, of course—and for every day of the rest of your life. That's the provision and the glory of El-Shaddai!

> All the way my Savior leads me,
> Cheers each winding path I tread,
> Gives me grace for every trial,
> Feeds me on the living bread.
>
> When my spirit cloth'd immortal
> Wings its flight to realms of day,
> This my song through endless ages,
> Jesus led me all the way.

6

Your Mountains are Moved

One day Jesus and His disciples were walking along the Bethany road on their way to Jerusalem. Jesus was hungry. On the hillside was a fig tree. The Master and His disciples went up to the tree to see if there were any figs on it. It had nothing but leaves. It was a fig tree without figs. So the Lord cursed it and declared that no man in the future would ever eat of its fruit, for never again would it bear any. *Now why did Jesus do that?* He knew there were no figs on it before He approached it. If He could see Nathaniel under the fig tree when he was out of sight, He could certainly see if the fig tree had any figs on it.

Jesus never did things without a purpose. There was a motive back of all His words and works. So there was a meaning in the incident. There was a lesson He wanted to bring to the disciples with Him, for had the incident been devoid of teaching, it never would have happened. There was a lesson He wanted to preserve for us, also, for if there hadn't been, the story would never have occupied precious space in the Bible. *What was the lesson, and why was it taught?*

The Lord continued into Jerusalem with His followers. Out of the temple He drove the merchandisers who were profaning His Father's house with their commercialism. The following day He and His disciples were back on the Bethany Road. Peter saw the fig tree. It was dead and withered. He was astounded and cried out, ""Rabbi, look! The fig tree which You cursed has withered away."

When Jesus answered, he spoke not to Peter alone, but to all of them—and to us. Here was the motive for cursing the fig tree—it was to help them and us better understand God and His ways in relation to us. "So Jesus answered and said to them, Have faith in God" (Mark 11:22).

Now here is that sentence in the order in which the words appear in my Greek New Testament—as you probably know, the structure of Greek sentences is different from that of our English sentences. Here's the word-for-word translation from the original Greek: "And answering, the Jesus says to them: 'Have you faith of God.'" Then the Master went on to tell them that if they had such a faith, not only could they dry up a fig tree, but they could command a mountain to be cast into the sea. The lesson was that of the irresistible power of the faith that was the faith *of God.* It was indeed mountain-moving faith.

One of the requirements for doing works of power, as you will see by reading the record in Mark 11:22-26, is that there be *no doubt in the heart* about the consummation of the miracle—nothing but a certainty that the thing you desire and pray for will happen. When those conditions are met, then the miracle—whatever it is—has to happen; for back of it is the Word of God, and back of His Word is His power—the same power that brought everything into existence at His command.

Most Bible versions translate Mark 11:22 as "Have faith *in* God," and that we interpret to mean that we are to have confidence in His ability to move a mountain. So we say to ourselves, "If I have faith enough in God, and can believe hard enough and get all doubt out of my heart, then God will move my mountain."

An Impossibility

You're trying to do the impossible. Your faith would never be great enough for that even if you struggled for a million years. What a mistake it is to take our belief in God and call it faith. Hundreds of thousands have struggled uselessly to believe for their healing because they haven't discerned the difference between belief in the power of God to heal and the faith of God that brings the victory. There's a great difference between the faith of man in God, and the faith of God that is imparted to man. Such faith is not the child of effort, and is it not born of struggle.

If it's the faith *of God,* then we get it from Him, and not from our mental attitudes or affirmations. Jesus did *not* say, "If you have the power to believe that God will remove that mountain, then He will do it." Neither did He say, "If you can believe hard enough that it is done, then it will be done." He said, "Have the faith *of* God." In other words, get a mustard seed of God's faith—and then you'll have the only power that can move mountains and cast them into the sea.

Now I know that in the second part of His statement He talks about believing with the heart and having no doubts. But the second part is impossible without the first part—you simply cannot believe without doubt until you have *the faith of God.* It takes God's faith to clear our human hearts of all anxieties, fears, and doubts.

As I've ministered to thousands of sick people over the years, I've learned that it's far more important to seek the

47

Healer than healing. In His presence there is a hiding place for the soul. As we empty ourselves of the world and its ways, we make room for the things that only God can impart. After our blessed Lord told His disciples about the faith that would move mountains, He told them to forgive everybody against whom they had any ill feelings. God cannot—or will not—impart His faith to us through a heart that is filled with bitterness and an unforgiving spirit.

I don't mean that He demands perfection of life and conduct before He imparts the grace of His faith, but perhaps there will be things that He *will* require of us before He will impart His blessings. A God of infinite and eternal love wants no malice in the hearts of His children. How can we, who have been forgiven so much, refuse to forgive those who perhaps have transgressed against us?—and sometimes they don't even know they have.

The Lord's meaning is clear. If we want to receive the faith that is the faith of God, then we must forgive all who trespass against us. When the soul cries out its need of God because of its own helplessness, it is into a *yielded heart* that His faith comes—and with it the consciousness that God's faith is there.

A Woman's Story

Some years ago a woman who needed healing came to our meetings. She seemed to be such a noble character, and her family loved her devotedly and dearly. One night we prayed for her in the name of the Lord Jesus, and she went away seemingly happy. She said she was standing on the promises of God—but she was not healed. As the days went by, two of her daughters came to see me, and begged me to pray again. They were almost hysterical in their anxiety and desperation. They loved their mother, and they knew that God was her only hope. They asked me to anoint her once again. I did.

I still remember the pleadings, the importunities, and the frantic cries of those dear people as they stormed the throne of grace. They tried to believe, but it seemed to be all in vain. The poor, sick, woman brushed away tears as we sang, "Jesus breaks every fetter," and went away from the meeting without any evident answer to our prayers. Two days passed. Then before the service she came to my office. Here was a different woman! Her face shone with an inner light.

"You've been healed!" I said.

She smiled and said, "No, not yet. But I shall be tonight. Because I was prayed for publicly, I believe my Lord wants to touch me by His power in the service tonight so that all may see that He's faithful." There was no tenseness about her now, just a sweet and beautiful rest in the Lord. Then she told me her story.

She had gone home from the previous meeting almost in despair. She had come to the end of herself and she knew it. As she knelt by the side of her bed and prayed, she sobbed, "Dear Jesus, I have tried so hard to have faith and I can't. I have failed, dear Lord, and yet I do believe in your promise and your Word. Brother Price has tried, and he has failed. The people in the meeting have tried and they, too, have failed. Where can I go? What can I do? Speak to me, Lord. My only hope is in Thee."

Then came the thought of a woman who had succeeded her as the teacher of a young people's class. Deep in her heart there had developed a feeling against that woman who had won the hearts of the young people whose love and affection had once been showered upon her. Was it envy? Was it jealousy? She didn't know—but she did know that over the months the feeling had gotten stronger. As thoughts of the incident filled her mind, she saw the true condition of her heart. Perhaps she heard the Master say, "And when ye stand praying, forgive."

The next day she spent an hour in prayer with the woman, and God put in her heart a strong love for her. The wounds

49

were healed, the envy melted away, and the love of Jesus flowed in. When she got home, she told her family that she would be healed that night. She knew it, but she did not know how she knew it. The consciousness of it was as real as life itself. There was no doubt about it. There was no intercession. That had been a work of the past. There was no agonizing and pleading. It was done—and yet it was not! That's the paradox of *real faith.*

Then she said to me, "My Brother, do you know what Jesus has done?"

"I know that my Lord doeth all things well," I replied.

"He has given me His faith," she said. "Honestly, I don't know the moment I received it; but, praise His name, I know it's here."

And it was. That night the Christ of the healing road touched the sick, weary body of His needy child. That night a cancer was melted by the touch divine. A mountain was moved by the faith of God that had been imparted to a sick woman by the Lord of glory Himself.

Seek the Healer, Not the Healing

Our problem is that we seek healing instead of the healer. Of what use is it to look for light and disdain the sun. The woman who had the issue of blood didn't struggle to be healed by mental effort. She just wanted to touch Jesus. All blind Bartimaeus did was crowd into his heart-rending cry the sound of his helplessness and his belief in the love, power, and compassion of Jesus of Nazareth. Even though our blessed Lord did tell him that it was *his* faith that had made him whole, I am sure that what faith he had was given him by the Lord Himself.

Can a man generate enough faith to find healing in walking a few feet on a dusty road? The presence of Jesus was the source of faith in those days, and it's the presence of Jesus that is the source of our faith in these days—even as Jesus said, "Without me, ye can do nothing."

True disciples of Jesus love to read the twelfth chapter of Romans. It raises wonderful possibilities in the standard of separated, consecrated, Christian living. It's the type of gospel, however, that carnal Christians don't like to contact. Paul is beseeching Christians to go on from good to better, and from there to better still. They're not to be conformed to this world, but transformed—literally, transfigured—by the renewing of their minds. The Greek word is *renovation* When you renovate a lawn, you rake out the old and put in the new. This renovation is necessary in Christian living before we can prove "what is that good and acceptable and perfect will of God" (Romans 12:2).

When that has happened, what then should be our attitude? Paul continues in his writing, "For I say, through the grace given unto me, to every man that is among you, not to think of himself more highly than he ought to think, but to think soberly, according as God hath dealt to every man the measure of faith." *God gives the faith—He measures it out!* The Greek New Testament reads, "To each one has the God divided a measure of faith." Weymouth's translation has it, "In accordance with the amount of faith which God has allotted to each one."

Do you not see how foolish we are to struggle and try to believe *mentally*, when we should believe *spiritually*? *Real faith* is of the heart—and only God can put faith in a heart. *Real faith* will accept the unreasonable—it believes what reason says is impossible. *Real faith* counts the things that are, as though they were not; and the things that are not, as though they were.

Faith put strength in Noah's arm to build for a hundred years, when there was no sign of flood. It sent an army marching around Jericho's walls, when reason says it would take tramping feet a million years to wear out the foundations. It pulled a nation to the edge of a deep and impenetrable sea, and opened its gates at Moses command. It sent men without flinching into furnaces of fire, and preserved them in the lion's den. Faith chased death away from its vigil over bodies, and it brought back the life that had fled. Faith! *God's Faith!* Not weak, puny struggles to believe, and not futile efforts to pull down omnipotent power.

Can a teacup contain an ocean? Can a grain of sand envelop a planet? Can our poor understanding comprehend the glory of an omnipotent God? Only as His love divine is freely given, only as He chooses to reveal Himself to us, can we understand, and then only in part, for our minds are incapable of understanding Him fully. Only as He gives His pardon, are we saved. Only as He imparts His strength, are we able to fight the good fight of faith. Only as He gives His love, can we love our enemies. Only as He lifts us, can we rise above the world of sorrow and sin. *Only as He imparts His faith— the only faith that can move mountains—can we have real faith.* Needy one, at the end of the 'Road of Self' you'll find Him waiting. The author and the finisher of your faith is waiting to meet you there. Back of you are the tears and the sorrows, the heartaches and the disappointments, but the sunlit trail where Jesus stands is bright and glorious with the light of His presence. Trust Him for His grace, rest upon His promises. He is the giver of every good and perfect gift, and He will not withhold from you the faith you need.

7

God Wants to Make It Easy

I believe it is easier to go to Christ, and to ask Him for the imparting of His Faith, than it is to try to work up and generate your own. It's true that in several instances, the Master mentioned the faith of the people who came to Him and were healed, and on occasions He complimented them because they had faith. My question is not whether or not they had it, but where did they get it?

Samson had strength. With it he accomplished superhuman feats of power. But where did he get it? He was a physical example of what we are admonished to be in a spiritual way. "Be strong in the Lord, and in the power of His might" (Ephesians 6:10). Paul continually acknowledged his weakness, and yet declared, "I can do all things through Christ which strengtheneth me" (Philippians 4:13).

Do you remember that wonderful incident in the twenty-first chapter of John about how the disciples had fished all night in their own strength and caught nothing. Then as they pulled in toward shore, a voice asked them, "Children, have ye any meat?" They had none. It was the risen Lord asking them and He knew, of course, that they had caught nothing even though they toiled throughout the night. "They answered Him, No." He told them to cast their net on the right side.

When they obeyed, their net was so full they could not pull it in. Following His instructions, they caught more fish in a minute than they caught in a whole night of their own efforts. It's a wonderful story, but the most wonderful and revealing part of it comes in Jesus' next statement.

Talk about generosity! Talk about benevolence and graciousness! He said "Bring of the fish which *ye* have now caught." Who caught those fish? Jesus said they did. But I ask you again, "Who caught those fish?" You know as well as I do who caught them. *It was Jesus! Yet He said that they caught them. Thus He speaks of our* faith, *our* love, and *our* this and that—as if we were anything at all apart from Him, and as if whatever we have had not come from Him. "A man can receive nothing, except it be given him from heaven" (John 3:27). "What hast thou that thou didst not receive? now if thou didst receive it, why dost thou glory, as if thou hadst not received it?" (1 Corinthians 4:7).

His Perfection

Mark 5:27-28 gives us a beautiful illustration of this great truth. Alexander Maclaren says, "The main part of this story seems to be the illustration which it gives of the genuineness and power of an imperfect faith, and Christ's merciful way of responding to and strengthening such a faith." Look at the woman. She allows Jesus to pass. Then, timid and shrinking, she crowds her way to a place where she can touch His robe. Does she believe some peculiar kind of magic is connected with His garment?

After the contact is made, she tries to lose herself in the crowd. The whole manner of her approach is evidence that she did not have what we habitually call faith—that *Bible faith* that moves mountains and heals sick bodies. She didn't ask Him to speak a word! Yet, in her misery and ignorance, she touched His robe and was instantly healed! Virtue (power) left Jesus to accomplish the miracle.

The whole message of the story is the fact that such healing is not dependent upon the development of a perfect faith by any processes of self at all, but rather depends on contact with Jesus, who is the author and finisher of our faith, and the giver of every good and perfect gift.

Let me again quote Dr. Maclaren:

> The power and vitality of faith is not measured by the comprehensiveness and clearness of belief. The richest soil may bear shrunken and barren ears; and on the arid sand with the thinnest layer of earth, gorgeous cacti may blossom out, and fleshy aloes lift their branches with stores of moisture to help them stand the heat. It is not for us to say what amount of ignorance is destructive to real confidence in Jesus Christ. But for ourselves, feeling how short a distance our sight travels and how little, after all, the great bulk of men in Christian lands know of theological truth, and how wide are the differences of opinion amongst us, and how soon we come to towering barriers beyond which our poor faculties can neither pass nor look, it ought to be a joy to us that a faith which is clouded with ignorance may yet be a faith which Christ accepts.

That's my point. Christ supplies the deficiency. He makes up the need. When Jesus came down from the mountain of His transfiguration, He found a despairing father and a group of impotent disciples trying to do by their faith what could be done only by the faith of the Son of God. The father was more honest than most of us when he said, "Lord I believe; help thou mine unbelief" (Mark 9:24). The scene of those disciples struggling, shouting, rebuking, and trying to cast out the devil—without success, has been duplicated thousands of times in our day. But when Jesus walked on the scene, how quickly and beautifully the entire atmosphere was changed and transformed.

Out of the storm there came calm, out of the tempest there came peace. Jesus was master of the situation, and happy was the father who beheld that day the approach of a tender, sympathetic heart that was moved with compassion.

The great essential is that we talk with Jesus, cease our efforts, and turn from our struggles to that trust and confidence in Him that will invite the imparting of the faith that He alone can give.

For over twenty years I've been conducting campaigns in which a prominent place has been given to prayer for the sick and the suffering. To this ministry my Lord has called me, and to that call I have responded with all my heart. To His glory and praise, I testify that I have seen miracles of divine power that have opened the eyes of the blind, raised the disabled and paralyzed from their wheelchairs and cots, and melted cancers and tumors by the healing power of our wonderful Lord.

During those years I've noticed that all great healing services have been preceded by nights of consecration and seasons of prayer. When the crowds have rushed forward seeking healing, the meetings have been hard and difficult. When they have sought the healer rather than the healing, however, the sweetness of His presence has broken the power of the enemy, and the sunshine of His presence has melted the icy feeling that gripped the heart. It may be self-pity, or even self-love, that brings us to His feet, but once we are there our whole viewpoint is changed as we at last see Him and Him alone.

The Poor and the Rich

It is the poor and the needy who have been given so many good things, and it is the rich whom He has sent away empty. A disabled man was brought to the meetings some years ago. Those who brought him told me he was a man possessed of all the faith in the world, loved the Lord, and was well known for his good life and works. Nevertheless, he was to leave many meetings unhealed because of the one thing that he lacked, and which his Master ultimately revealed to him.

How the people prayed for that man! I can see him now, struggling to rise in answer to the entreaties of the people that he arise in faith and walk. Many times I knelt by the side of his chair and rebuked the power that bound him. Yet days went by and he was not healed. One afternoon they wheeled him to a corner in the building. He asked the people to leave the two of us alone, and then said something that has lingered all these years in my mind.

"What a failure I am," he declared. " I came here strong in what I thought was my faith in the Lord. But now as I look deeply into my heart I find something I wish to confess. What a poor, miserable, failure I have been. I've been spiritually proud of the fact that people have pointed to me as a man who suffered without complaining. They pointed me out as the man who never grumbled, although he had a cross to bear. I grew proud of my reputation, and I can see now that what I termed my goodness has been self-righteousness in the sight of my Lord."

He put his face into his hands and wept. There was something so pathetic about that poor man that the tears welled up in my eyes too. I put my hands on his head and started to pray for his healing, but he stopped me. "Dr. Price," he said, "I don't need healing half as much as I need Jesus. I'm so hungry for His presence. More than anything else in my life, I want to know Him better, and I'm content to spend my days in this chair if only He will flood this self-righteous heart of mine with His peace and love." He went away quietly, and my heart went with him as I watched them wheel him out of the building. All the way home my heart sang for him:

> Savior, Savior, hear my humble cry;
> While on others Thou art calling,
> Do not pass me by!

Psalm 51:17 says that a broken and a contrite heart He will not despise. How sweet it is to come to the end of self. How wonderful, after we have toiled all night and have caught nothing, that He waits for us on the shore. How gracious the voice that tells us to cast our nets on the right side of the boat, that our joy might be full! What determines which is the right side of a boat? Why, the way it is going, of course. You'll soon find out where the right side is if your boat is going toward Jesus—and, remember, the boat must be empty if you would bring the Nazarene on board.

A few days later I was leaving the building in company with Dr. Manchester, the man who buried President McKinley. At the door of the auditorium sat the man in his wheelchair, patiently waiting for the doors to open for the evening service. The afternoon meeting was over. Dr. Manchester looked at the face of the man and stopped. Then he walked over to him and I followed. "Are you coming for prayer?" he asked.

"For prayer and to receive healing," was the reply. There was something different about the man. His voice, his tone, his eyes—there was a look of reflected glory on his face. I knew something had happened. "Tell me," I said, "What's happened. I can tell you've experienced something that is so wonderful I can feel its glory, though I don't know what it is."

Then he told me he had been with Jesus. He had spent the night in prayer—not in intercession alone, but in praise and worship. He told me that at four in the morning a consciousness of the presence of his Lord had overwhelmed him. He knew Jesus was in his room in a special way. He told me how he offered adoration to his Lord, and how he became conscious of *an infusion of divine life into him.* Something passed from Jesus to him, and he felt as though a fog had rolled away from his heart and mind. From that moment on he knew his struggles were over, and a sweet and holy peace wrapped around his soul. He told us he knew that when he came again to obey his Lord and be anointed with oil, power would flow from Jesus and restore him to health and strength.

Tears rolled down Dr. Manchester's face, and he asked, "Why does this man have to wait until tonight?"

"He doesn't," I replied. "The Great Physician is here now. Jesus of Nazareth is passing by."

A moment later it was over. Out of his wheelchair rose that man. He ran and jumped and praised the Lord for his deliverance. It was a miracle of power divine. Around him on the snowy street, men and women gathered to praise and to pray. Unsaved hearts were broken, and many penitent tears were shed.

More than once I have been with a group of disciples, struggling at the foot of a mountain; and oh, how my heart can testify to the difference it makes when into the midst of our helplessness Jesus Himself comes down from the mountain of heaven.

Your Prayers Answered

Don't you know that your prayers can be answered? Don't you know that your burdens and cares can be left at His feet—

that you never need bow your shoulders again with the weight of sorrow and care? I am praying, please God, that thousands will read these lines and abandon their self-efforts as they realize that it has led them only into doubts and fears that destroy confidence and trust in God.

Know ye not that "faith cometh by hearing, and hearing by the word of God" (Romans 10:17)? In my Greek New Testament it reads, "and hearing by a word of God." There is a finer ear than the one with which we listen to church music. There is clearer ear than the one we use to listen to the reading of the grand old Book. The Bible is a book through which God speaks, but all do not hear His voice in the lines.

"Faith cometh by hearing, and hearing by *a word of God.*" Let Jesus speak to your heart and doubts will fly away on the wings of the morning. Let Jesus breathe a little word to your burdened mind and heaven is brought to earth. Fear is gone like a shadow in the light of His glorious truth. Let Him say, "Bring him to me," and then cometh faith—God's faith—His faith—and the weary heart will cry, "Lord, that I may receive my sight." Let Jesus breathe on you with His love and presence, and your mountains will tremble and race for the ocean.

That's how faith comes! Not through the channels of human concepts. Not along the paths of human understandings. Not by the ability of the mind to understand, or the power of the intellect to affirm. Reach for your healing with those and you'll struggle endlessly in vain to obtain it. But let Jesus speak, and it will be enough. Just one word from Jesus is worth more than all the words in all the dictionaries there have ever been or will ever be.

There is hope for every Bartimaeus on today's Jericho Road when Jesus of Nazareth is passing their way. "Hope," did I say? Yes, hope—and more than hope; for when He hears our cry of helplessness, He will not pass us by. When He speaks, hope is kindled until it becomes a fire that burns away all doubt and unbelief, and the warmth of a divine and beautiful faith brings healing to the soul and body.

> *O Master, speak! In our need and self-helplessness, we would lift our hearts and voices to Thee. Speak the word—that will be all we need. We have tried, with the broken cisterns of our faith and endeavors, to believe; but their waters have failed!*

> Savior, Savior, hear my humble cry;
> While on others Thou art calling,
> Do not pass me by!

8

Imparted Faith

My heart is joyful because I know that my Lord is able to supply all our need. The quantity of His grace is so abundant toward us that it is inconceivable to our earthbound minds. We deal with the limited and temporal, while God deals with the unlimited and eternal. God always gives to overflowing abundance. The apostle stated, "Who giveth to all men liberally," and there is no end to His beneficence, or His inexhaustible supply. He has promised time and again that He would open the windows of heaven to heart-faith. In light of that, it's tragic that so many live in spiritual poverty. We need to take a closer look at what the Bible calls *faith*.

Faith is the quality or power by which the things desired become the things possessed. It's the substance of things hoped for, the evidence of things not seen. That's the nearest to a definition of what faith is—even in the inspired Word. In spite of its potency, faith is an intangible commodity. You can't see it, weigh it, or measure it. It's like trying to define energy in one comprehensive statement.

We're told that the atom is a world within itself, and that the potential energy contained within its tiny universe is so great that it bewilders the mind. [Editor's note: At the time Dr. Price wrote this book, the atomic bomb had not been developed and nuclear energy was unknown to the public.] But attempt to define it and you'll run into difficulties. Faith is like that. There have been times when I have felt it stealing over my soul until I have dared to say and do things that, had I allowed reason to take charge, I would never have said and done. Though the faith may have come only as big as a mustard seed, it flowed through word and act with irresistible power, until people looked in wonder upon the mighty works of the Lord.

One thing I do know—one thing I've learned— *I cannot produce faith.* In neither me nor you are there any spiritual ingredients that can be mixed together to make even a mustard seed of real Bible faith. Since this is true, aren't we foolish to try to bring about results without *real faith?* If I want to cross a lake and find there is no way to reach the other side except by boat, wouldn't it be foolish of me to struggle to get across without a boat? *The thing I should seek is the boat—not the other side of the lake!* Get the boat, and it will take you there.

There are many things that we receive by faith and only by faith—the Word clearly states this time and again. But all the *things* are on the other side of the lake. So where do we get the faith that will take us across our "lakes"? Scriptures tell us that faith is a gift of God or a fruit of the Spirit. Whether it's a gift or fruit, the source of faith is the same. *It comes from God!* There is no other source of *real faith*—for it is the "faith of God."

Now let's suppose that faith was something *we* possessed. Considering its power, it would be a dangerous possession. Suppose we could use it to cross the "lake" when God wanted us on this side? Suppose you or I had faith enough this morning to raise up every sufferer among us. If we were to utilize such power, how do we know but what we might be opposing God's will or overthrowing a divine plan?

An Example of the Danger

Some time ago a lady brought a sick little girl to me. She was a sweet tot, pretty as a picture, quiet and retiring—and seriously ill. The girl's father loved her dearly, but was rebellious against God . For years his wife prayed for him to surrender, but he always had some excuse. Three times they brought their daughter for prayer—had there been real faith she would have been healed, but she wasn't.

The mother went to prayer! Later she called me and said, "Dr. Price, I feel that God is dealing with my husband. He loves our little girl so much that I think the Lord can reach his heart through her. Wouldn't be wonderful if I could get him to come with us when you pray once again? Perhaps, if we could get him on his knees to pray for his daughter, it wouldn't be long before he would be praying for himself."

The next time they came for prayer, he came along. He was courteous, kind, and solicitous about his little girl; but when I asked him to pray, he said, "No, I don't want to be a hypocrite."

The Holy Spirit spoke through me and I said, "Brother, get on your knees, and let us look to the Lord together. If you do, I believe you will take a little girl home who has been healed by the touch of the Savior's hand."

He looked at me in amazement and said, "Do you ready believe that?" I told him I did. He dropped to his knees! When he did, there sweetly stole over the body of the little girl the healing virtue of Jesus, and she raised her expressive eyes to God in a prayer of thanksgiving and gratitude. At the same time, the father gave his heart to the Savior, and another soul entered the kingdom of God.

Suppose I had possessed faith enough and could have used it at will. Would that have brought as much glory to the name of the Lord as the imparted faith that was given at the time it was needed—and would the sins of a heart-hungry father been forgiven? I think not.

Many years ago, while I was in a campaign in Vancouver, B. C., an incident occurred that kept me awake most of the night with my heart open before the Lord. I had prayed for hundreds that night, and there was a real consciousness in the meeting of the sweet and wonderful presence of the Savior. Many weary bodies had been renewed by the Master's hand. They had received deliverance from their pains and sicknesses as they knelt at the foot of the Cross. Dr. Gabriel Maguire, pastor of the First Baptist Church, was there, and I turned to him said, "The Lord is imparting faith tonight. The power of the Lord is present to heal." He replied that he had never been more conscious of the moving power of God in all his life.

A minute later, we both placed our hands on the head of a man at the altar. A feeling like a vacuum came over me. I felt drained and empty. *The presence of the Lord was with me, but I had no confidence or faith to pray for the man, and nothing happened to him.* I prayed again. The emptiness increased, and I was about to cry out to the Lord and ask why He seemed to have departed when He had been so sweetly manifest just before. But, instead, I turned to the man and said, "Brother, why are you here? Who are you? What is the purpose of your coming to the platform?"

He turned pale. Then he made a confession, He said he was a professional hypnotist. He had argued with people and told them that the power in the meeting was the power of hypnotism, and decided to use himself as a test case so he could prove it. Then he planned to hold a public meeting and expose the whole divine healing movement.

Now this man actually was sick—he did need healing. But suppose I had possessed faith for him. It would have been disastrous to have brought healing to that man. Fortunately, I didn't possess the faith to do it. How do I know? *If the thing we call faith is powerless, it isn't real faith.* You can't have real faith without results any more than you can have motion without movement.

The thing we sometimes call faith is simply trust. We trust in the Lord, but faith has feet and wings and power. *A person could not have faith for salvation and not be saved.* Isn't that so? Someone could trust the Lord and promise that someday he would come to Christ,—but when he has *faith for salvation*, it means *he is saved.*

So it was with the man whose case I just recounted. Whatever faith was given during the evening was withdrawn from me until I was praying for someone, who in the providence and will of God, was ready to receive the blessing He alone can impart. It so happened that the next person we prayed for was a woman who received one of the most miraculous healings of the entire campaign.

Now no Christian is entirely devoid of faith. Enough faith is implanted in the heart to maintain your salvation, obey the Lord, and do the things that are pleasing in His sight—but you are continually dependent upon Him for its perpetuity. You cannot keep the light and dismiss the sun. You cannot have *faith in God unless you have the faith of God.* That's why the Scripture says, "By grace are ye saved, through faith; and that *not of yourselves*; it is *the gift of God*" (Ephesians 2:8).

Grace and faith are so closely related that they can't be separated. The wonder of it is that faith is often imparted when we feel the least deserving. The gift of faith is the beautiful flower of grace. It's seldom a product of merit. We dare not say for a moment that it was because of our deeds and words that the faith needed to lift us out of our pains and sufferings was given to us. The faith that was suddenly yours in your hour of trial, how did it come, and why? When I survey the wondrous Cross, I begin in part to understand why grace smiles on faith as it goes on every mission and ministry of life.

What Manner of Man?

The disciples and the Master are in a boat on the stormy waters of Galilee. Just a few moments before the sea had been tranquil, but now a tempest throws their small boat about. They're terrified at the raging waves and ferocious winds, even as you and I would be. How quickly the scenes of life can change. It doesn't take long for laughter to be drowned in tears, and a happy heart torn by sorrow. Perhaps the incident of the Galilee storm can teach us what God intended it to teach.

"Jesus was asleep in the boat, and the disciples woke Him and said, Master, master, we perish" (Luke 8:23). He rose and "rebuked the wind and the raging of the water: and they ceased, and there was a calm." Then he turned to His disciples and asked, "Where is your faith?"

Yes, where was it? Had it fallen overboard? Had it been blown away by the wind? Had it dissolved in the spray that washed their boat? No, none of these, for their Faith was with them all the time. *They made the mistake of ignoring the fact of His presence, while discerning the fact of the storm!* He later told them, "Without me ye can do nothing," and He had just shown them exactly that.

Do you not know? Can you not see? Their faith was just as near to them as He is to you and me, for the fact of the storm doesn't mean He's gone. *The storm in your life may be just a wind blowing a miracle your way.* It may be God's method of making you say, "What manner of man is this, that even the wind and the seas obey Him?"

Can you imagine Peter standing in that boat telling those waves to be still? I can—if the Master of the sea had imparted faith for the miracle. It was Peter who confidently said to the man at the gate Beautiful, "Such as I have, give I unto thee," and proved that he had *real faith.* The man was healed, and he followed Peter and John into the Temple, shouting the praises of God. But where did Peter get the faith? To find out, all we have to do is look at what Peter said:

> And when Peter saw it, he answered unto the people, Ye men of Israel, why marvel ye at this? or why look ye so earnestly on us, as though by our own power or holiness we had made this man to walk?
> And his name through faith in his name hath made this man strong, whom ye see and know: yea, *the faith which is by him* hath given him this perfect soundness in the presence of you all.
> (Acts 3:12, 16, italics added)

[Editor's note: Bible versions that have appeared since the first publication of this book, such as the NIV and the NKJV, clarify verse 16 and add authority to Dr. Price's teaching of imparted faith:

> (Acts 3:16 NIV, italics added.) . . . *the faith that comes through him* that has given this complete healing to him, as you can all see.

> (Acts 3:16 NKJV, italics added.) ". . . Yes, *the faith which comes through Him* has given him this perfect soundness in the presence of you all."]

What a vast difference between this truth and our feeble attempts to transfer faith from the heart to the mind, to turn faith from a grace-imparted quality to an intellectual belief, and to look for it in the power of our wills rather than in the light of Christ that streams from heaven. There's an ocean of difference between the disabled person who struggles and tries to walk, and the one who looks and prays for the faith by which he will walk. I know from many testimonies that such faith is given while the soul waits before God in a quiet and beautiful attitude of trust and rest in His promises, rather than in the turbulent atmosphere of our noisy strivings and endeavors. "Wait, I say, on the Lord. Rest in the Lord! Wait patiently for Him and He shall bring it to pass." (See Psalm 37.)

On the raging Sea of Galilee, the disciples faith was not far away. He slept awhile to teach them to rely upon Him. He slept so that confidence in self might be turned to trust in His promise and in the power of His presence. Your faith is not far away either. Look to Him in trust and confidence, and His voice will whisper to your troubled heart and tell you that if He can rest in the midst of the tempest and the storm, then you can sweetly rest in Him.

9

Faith Is a Gift

Faith is one of two things—it's either a gift of God or a fruit of the Spirit. Of that there's no doubt. The reason why faith cannot be of us is clear. If faith "as a grain of mustard seed" contains the power that can move mountains, then God cannot entrust to us a weapon that potent. If He did, He would put into the hands of weak people like you and I a power that would destroy us.

It's not only that we would use faith for the wrong things, but it would seriously damage out dependent relationship to God and impede our spiritual growth. More than once I've tried to exercise faith, and have struggled to obtain the prayer-answer I desired, only to find out later that it was far better that the prayer wasn't answered in the way I wanted.

That's why God gives us only the measure of faith we need to walk in harmony with His will. Beyond that point, faith is not imparted. Many times I don't understand the purposes of God, but I trust Him and hold on when He doesn't impart faith. Whatever the reason He doesn't, I know He's working in my life for the very best.

We must trust Him when we can't see, and rely upon Him when we can't understand. But that trust isn't faith. Faith works dynamically and accomplishes things according to its measure and power. God measures faith much like we measure things on earth. Jesus talked about *little* faith, *great* faith, *weak* faith, *strong* faith, and *no* faith. When we need something that is God's will, faith is imparted by the Lord so that God's will be done on earth as it is in Heaven. The Christian world looks to the life of George Muller as a latter-day example of the power of faith in a man who believed God. In reading his biography, however, have you not noticed that he knew he was in the center of God's will? There were hungry little mouths to feed and small bodies to clothe. Muller believed that the Lord had called him to that ministry and would supply *every* need. And he was right—when a need arose, faith was given. There was no struggle, no agonizing, no battle against doubt—only the manifestation of an imparted faith.

Mueller was an ardent believer in fervent, effectual prayer. Many times he reveals the depth of his ministry of intercession. He says that so many people fail to have their prayers answered because they haven't learned importunity and continuity in prayer. Yet whenever he had a crisis, he would tell the Lord his need and believe it was done. It was almost as simple as calling up the grocery store and asking for the delivery of food. During the years he cared for the orphans, he received *over 50,000 recorded answers to specific prayers.*

Can you have faith like that in yourself? Impossible! Only God can impart such faith. Let me illustrate what I mean by imparted faith.

The Master Knew

It was during a healing service in Medford, Oregon, some years ago. The place was so crowded that some were even sitting on the ledges of the open windows. One of them was a little boy who walked with crutches. There was such a look of helplessness in his blue eyes that my heart was stirred. Silently I lifted my heart to the Lord and asked for faith for his healing.

About then a little girl stood in front of me for prayer. Her mother was weeping. I laid my hands on her head and prayed. Nothing happened, but the spirit of the meeting changed. There was a sudden deadness that weighed heavily upon me. I prayed again, and the feeling increased. I looked at the weeping mother in bewilderment. She was sobbing. At last she cried out, almost hysterically, "Why won't Jesus heal my girl?"

"Where do you worship?" I asked.

"I go to the Methodist Church," was her reply.

There was something about her answer that bothered me. At that moment the Lord imparted the gift of discernment to the person next to me, and she asked the woman, "Have you ever been in mysticism or occultism?"

She confessed she had. Instead of the Methodist Church, she had been attending a spiritualist seance for weeks. Then I knew why my Lord had withheld His blessing and His faith. The mother cried aloud, "He has healed others, please ask Him to heal my little girl."

I said, "Sister, do you know anything about salvation through the shed blood of Jesus on Calvary?"

She said she had at one time, but a sorrow had come into her life and, instead of taking a tighter grip on the hand divine, she had turned away from God. In response to my appeal, she said that she would like to give her heart to Christ then and there, and asked me to pray for her. She prayed a prayer of repentance and surrender after me, and then I closed with the words, "I am trusting in Jesus as my personal Savior, and I claim the promise of the blood as the atonement for all my sin."

As the woman surrendered to Christ, into my heart and hers came a glory wave from heaven. As I reached out my hand once again to her little girl, I knew that her days in a wheelchair were over. She sprang to her feet, totally healed! Then I looked at the little boy and held out my hand for him to try to climb through the window and come to the platform for prayer. He didn't climb through, he fell through, leaving his crutches on the outside! He, too, was marvelous healed.

The Holy Ghost took such charge of that service, that I have seldom seen anything to equal it. Not only were people healed, but many were saved. Down the aisle came a dear old lady who had been in a wheelchair for years. She was leaping, shouting, and praising God. What a meeting! What a time to make men adore Him and angels to rejoice.

Now, suppose I had possessed faith for the healing of that little girl. Suppose that when I first laid hands on her head, she had gone away well. Her mother would have taken it as a sign that attending seances was in the will of God, and from that moment on she would have been more deeply entrapped in spiritism. So when I prayed in my lack of understanding, the spirit of faith and assurance was lifted from me. How empty I felt. Then, when the mother received Jesus as her personal savior, faith was imparted and the work was done.

This is what I'm trying to show you—instead of struggling to be healed, how much sweeter and richer life will be when we learn to look to Jesus who is "the author and the finisher of our faith."

A Happy Morning

One morning, some years ago, I went to pray for a poor woman who had lost her mind, and was confined in an institution. I can still hear her husband's sobs and desperate cry. Disaster had struck their beautiful home without warning. God was their only hope, and the husband knew it. I was anxious to pray for that woman and had gone forth confident that the Lord would hear and answer prayer. She was in such a helpless condition, and in the grip of an evil spirit! When at last I arrived at her room, she shouted blasphemies and obscenities in a voice that wasn't her own.

That morning we saw no visible answer to our prayers, so I called my church to prayer—and called other churches too. We all agreed to pray for an entire day for the woman's deliverance, and several prayer warrior resolved to stay on their knees until the woman was delivered.

About four o'clock that afternoon, while praying near the altar of the church, I felt the Spirit of the Lord come upon me. Under the impulse of that anointing, and trembling with emotion and the glory of His presence, I announced that our prayers had gotten through, and that the answer we desired was on the way. I called the husband and told him that I believed we had received the victory. We had!

The following day, after a brief season of prayer and anointing, the woman arose in victory and triumph, and went home once again to her adoring husband and children. I knew the moment at which the evil spirit released his grip upon her poor soul and left her body.

I was conscious that the faith of Christ had been given—released—at that moment of victory. I could not release His faith myself—if I could have, in my limited understanding of God's purpose, she would have been healed the first time I prayed. But it was not until the Lord released in me the faith he had imparted in love and grace, that the miracle of healing took place. Our possession of miracle-working faith is always subject not only to His imparting but also to His control.

A woman said to me the other day, "Pray for me, please. I have all the faith in the world." I knew what she meant. We hear that expression so many times. My reply was, "Sister, if you have that much faith, why are you sick?" She looked at me strangely. Then, after a few moments of thought, she went away to pray for faith "as a grain of mustard seed."

During the years of campaigns in Canada and the United States, God's grace has privileged me to pray for as many as ten thousand people in a single month. Those many meetings have stamped some experiences indelibly on the mind. In a meeting the atmosphere would be tense and hard, prayer would seem to be in vain, and our efforts to bring victory would meet with seeming failure. Then a sweep of glory and a rush of the power of the Holy Spirit would carry the meeting to the gates of Heaven. Such meetings have emphasized the great truth that I believe in ourselves we are helpless before "the powers of the air," and for miracles of healing to take place there must be a manifestation of the presence of the Lord.

"Without me," said the Savior, "you can do nothing."

We sometimes reply foolishly, "Oh but I can, for I have the faith. I can use it, exercise it, and bring things to pass with it, for the Word says that if we have faith, we can move mountains."

To such, I would say, "Go ahead, try it, and see what happens."

All things are possible to them that believe. But it is important *what* you believe. To believe that you, apart from grace and divine imparting, are the possessor of a power that can remove mountains is dangerous indeed. I know many who have believed that way and tried to exercise such power, but sorrow was their lot instead of joy.

The Vicar's Daughter

There was a meeting some years ago in Winnipeg that I shall never forget. Assisting in the campaign was a dear friend, Archdeacon Fair, of the Anglican Church. He brought one of his Vicars to the meeting. With them was the Vicar's sick daughter—she had been sent home from a hospital in America to die. They had given up on her.

The poor girl was in such excruciating pain that she had to take large quantities of opiates in order to live at all, for her suffering was beyond endurance. She sat just in front of the platform in a large chair—cushioned and surrounded by pillows. The building was filled with people, and with the presence of the Lord.

Toward the close of the service, I felt a familiar feeling come into my heart. I was literally melted in the Lord's presence. I turned to a minister near me and said, "The Lord is in this place and I think He is going to work a miracle tonight that will shake this meeting with the manifestation of His power." No sooner had I said those words, than I felt an imparting of faith for the sick woman.

I didn't hesitate. Stepping over to the side of Archdeacon Fair, I asked him to pray with me for the Vicar's daughter. He grasped my hand and said, "My Brother, I can feel the presence of Jesus in this meeting in a way I have never felt Him before in all my life. I feel that He will work this miracle tonight." He did!

Jesus laid his hands upon the sick body of the girl, and we could see the flush of health come back to her cheeks. She did not die, she lived—and she lives today as a living testimony to the power of our wonderful Lord.

A year later, when I visited that same building once again, I stood on the very spot where the Lord visited me that night. As I stood there, I remembered what I had been doing and what had happened at the moment He imparted to me the faith that my poor heart lacked. That's why I say that faith is a gift of God. You do not possess it to use at will, but for the purpose for which He gives it and permits you to keep it.

Let me repeat. He gives us the necessary faith for all things that are in accordance with His blessed will. That faith is first given and then grows as a fruit of the Spirit. But for the mountain-moving faith that banishes disease and sweeps away all barriers by miraculous power, I still maintain that such faith is possible only when it is imparted, and that when it is the Savior's will.

So put all your trust in Jesus, for only as you contact Him can you drink in the sweetness of His presence and receive the *real faith* that only He can give. Trust Him when such faith is withheld, and praise Him when it is given. Remember that "He doeth all things well."

You and I would blunder and err along the pathway if it were not for His restraining hand, as well as His bountiful provisions for our every need. The things that seem good to you today, could be your sorrows tomorrow. So how much better it is to let Him have His way with you, than to always try to have your way with Him. And what greater joy can there be than the possession of that faith which is "the faith of God!"

10

Faith Is a Fruit

Christian experience is a great adventure. We never reach the end of the trail. No matter what mountain peak we climb today, there's always another one to be climbed tomorrow. The future is greater than the past, for there are mountains of glory that have never been explored. It's this great truth that presents such a challenge to a follower of the Lord Jesus. Under His leadership we're privileged to climb in spirit close to the gates of a world that human eyes cannot see. It's there we begin to comprehend the incomprehensible, and have unfolded to us the mysteries that are hidden to so many.

There is one truth the Bible speaks with no uncertain voice—spiritual things are discerned only with the mind of the Spirit. The finite mind of man is incapable of understanding God and the things of God. We are the created and He is the

Creator, and there is an impassable region between us. The only door that opens the way from one to the other is Jesus Christ—and the only way to understand or approach God is through the Lord. He said of Himself, "I am the door; no man comes to the Father but by me."

Yet man continually tries intellectually to understand God and to reach Him by self-efforts. Because of his limited, finite understanding, he constantly turns "salvation by grace, through faith," into a salvation by conduct. He puts the emphasis upon what he does rather than what he is. In his sight, therefore, character is the "cross" upon which self is crucified—but upon such a cross the baser instincts simply twist and turn but never die. As a result, the Cross on which the Savior died is deemed unnecessary and obsolete.

It's for the same reasons that natural man has made faith a product of a finite mind, when all of the other fruits of the Spirit he has attributed to God. To many Christians, faith is still their own ability to believe a promise or a truth, and is often based on their struggles to drive away doubt and unbelief through a process of continuous affirmations—confessing over and again that they have what they prayed for.

Haven't we said, "I am going to believe that it's done, and if I can believe it's done, then it will be done?" Haven't we looked at a promise, and then struggled with all our mental might to bring about the result by our own ability to believe? Recently a poor, deluded, man, who undoubtedly loved his Lord, stuck his hand into a basket of snakes to prove his faith in God. For weeks he lingered between life and death. He came through all right, but it was a regrettable incident. He no doubt believed God, but what he called faith was only sinful presumption.

Some years ago, I had a long conversation with one of the secretaries of Pandita Ramabai, who was a beloved spiritual leader in India. She told me the story of how the "cobras came to Mukti" just after a glorious visitation of the Holy Spirit upon the girls in the home and school. The cobras appeared during the night and bit many of the girls in the compound. For a moment there was great fear, but then the Spirit of the Lord imparted faith for the emergency, and instead of cries of anguish and pain, there were shouts of victory and praise. Not a girl died from the deadly bites—everyone was healed. The imparted faith of God delivered them and brought them through.

There is belief in faith, but faith is more than belief! There is a rock on the mountain, but the mountain is more than the rock. Should the rock assert that it is the mountain, then I would say to it, "You are presuming too much." The truth that should be emphasized is this: *faith cannot be produced by mixing together various mental ingredients.* A tablespoon of confidence, an extra pinch of trust, an ounce of belief—plus a few other things—will *not* produce the faith that moves mountains. You are nearest to the manifestation of this imparted grace when you realize your own helplessness and total dependence upon the Lord!

The Love of God

Galatians 5:22 states that faith is part of the fruit of the Spirit. I say "part" because all the qualities Paul listed comprise the "fruit" of the Spirit—not fruits as many say, but fruit. Let's consider some of the other qualities. First, there is love. Whose love is it with which we love? Has our natural love been cleaned up and made over into something holy? No! It's the love of God shed abroad in the heart by the Holy Ghost. (See Romans 5:5.) It's God's wonderful love that fills the heart, and only His love makes it possible for us to love our enemies

When Stephen was stoned, what made him cry, "Lord, lay not this sin to their charge"? It wasn't said for effect. Neither was it just a heroic action in a moment of crisis. It was the love of God shed abroad in his heart by the Holy Spirit that enabled him to bless his murderers. It was God's love flowing through Stephen's heart like a river from the throne of grace. On the Cross, it was love that caused Jesus to say, "Father, forgive them, for they know not what they do" (Luke 23:34). At that moment, the love of Heaven in Jesus paid earth a little visit— and it did again when Stephen was stoned.

It wasn't by chance that Jesus and Stephen said almost the same thing. Stephen wasn't trying to imitate his Master, and neither was Jesus holding Himself up as only an example for believers to struggle to emulate. They both said the same thing because both had the same love. It was God's love in both hearts. Jesus had it because He was God—Stephen had it because Christ lived in him.

Human love can be improved, but a person could live a million years and never improve it enough to equal the love of God. How do we get God's love? God gives it, and the Spirit imparts it.

That's how we get the love of God, and that's how we get the faith of God.

Joy From the Hills

Joy is listed second in the fruit of the Spirit. What is this joy? Is it dependent upon our environment and circumstance? How do we get joy?

Some years ago I was a speaker in a campmeeting in an area where many of the people were poverty-stricken. One night before the service, I went for a drive to get away from people so I could meditate awhile before preaching. About five miles from the camp I saw a man and a woman with four children come out of the woods and start up the road. They were all barefoot, and carrying their shoes—those who had them—the four youngest children did not. I stopped my car and hailed them. Smiling but bashful, they accepted my offer of a ride. They were on their way to the campmeeting. At the gates of the camp the father and mother and oldest child put on their shoes. They were so grateful and humble about having been given a ride, that I managed to be at the woods to meet them every night for the rest of the campmeeting.

After the strangeness and bashfulness wore off, every night on the way to the service they would testify and sing, and sing and testify. Their joy was so abundant that it was a tonic to my soul. It helped me to preach better. From our talks, I learned that they carried their shoes to save the leather from wearing out on the concrete road, that they were poorer than any people I had ever known, and that they lived many miles back in the mountains. I also learned that they were richer by far than many who lived in great houses and who had more than enough of the possessions of this fleeting world.

One night, toward the end of the camp, I said to the father, "Perhaps, my brother, the day will come when the Lord will give you a better and larger home. You know that He often prospers us temporally as well as spiritually. The Bible says that . . . ."

The brother interrupted me. A smile of happiness came across his face and he started singing:

> A tent or a cottage, why should I care?
> They're building a palace for me over there;
> Though exiled from home, yet still I may sing,
> All glory to God, I'm a child of the King.

The little folks helped him sing it, and his good wife sang it too. When he finished, he said, "Brother Price, you never need to tell me that I got to have a big house to make me happy. If the Lord gives it to me, then I will thank Him, but I have something in my heart I wouldn't sell for all the money in the world. It's the joy of the Holy Ghost."

That's what I mean. You cannot get up in the morning and say, "This is the day in which I will be full of joy. I'm going to be very happy today, for I have made up my mind to have lots of joy." Either you have it, or you don't. The worldly man can have the synthetic joy that's the plaything of environment and the slave of circumstance. But Christians can have imparted joy in the Holy Ghost, and have it flow through them no matter what the conditions of life are like. Such joy isn't dependent upon surroundings, nor is it the slave of circumstance—it's the gift of God!

Peace, Perfect Peace

Third on Paul's list is peace. What a wonderful day it was for the disciples when Jesus said, "My peace I give unto you!" It wasn't to be the peace that the world knows—for that peace is false, weak, and flimsy, and can be lashed into a storm at any moment by the blowing winds of trouble.

The peace He gives passes all human understanding. (See Philippians 4:7.) It's so deep that no surface troubles can ever affect it, so divine that no human hand can ever reach it to take it away, and so full it touches every part of the soul. It's the peace Jesus had when He "held his peace" before the high priest when they accused Him of blasphemy. (See Matthew 26:23.)

Let me ask you, "Can you create that peace? Can you bring it about by a switch in mental attitude, a change in outlook, or some method or formula?" Of course not! There's only one way to get it:

> Be careful for nothing; but in every thing by prayer and supplication with thanksgiving let your requests be made known unto God.

84

And the peace of God, which passeth all
understanding, shall keep your hearts and minds through
Christ Jesus.

(Philippians 4:6-7)

It's God's peace, imparted by His Spirit. All we have to
do is cast all our cares and needs upon Him and receive His
peace while we wait for His answer. That's the beauty of the
Christ-centered life—a life that is hid with Christ in God.

So it is with faith. He doesn't give it as a plaything to be
operated for our own undoing and in things otherwise contrary
to His will. He knows my need. He knows yours, too—and
He has given His promise that "no good thing will He withhold
from them who walk uprightly" (Psalm 84:11). So we rest in
that promise and abide in Him, even as He abides in us. (See
John 15:4.)

To know that He is present and understands and cares, is
sufficient for me to know the joy that springs eternal in the
knowledge that "all things work together for good to them
that love God, to them that are the called according to His
purpose" (Romans 8:28). In the development of His will in
your life, let me assure you that when faith is needed, it will
not be withheld—for the Giver of every good gift and perfect
gift is the author and finisher of our faith.

11

The Vessel Made of Clay

The redemptive work of Christ covers the *complete person*—body, soul, and spirit. It even covers physical necessities. Jesus said, "Take no (anxious) thought, saying, What shall we eat? or, What shall we drink? or, Wherewithal shall we be clothed? for your heavenly Father knoweth that ye have need of all these things. But seek ye first the kingdom of God, and His righteousness; and all these things shall be added unto you" (Matthew 6:31-34). These are direct and definite statements—our heavenly Father knows what we need and promises that He will supply what we need.

Because there is such a close link between the spiritual and the natural, His disciples were not to seek the natural, but seek the spiritual. They were first to find the Kingdom, enter it, and there find an abundance that would meet every need of their lives. *That's the direct promise of our Lord!*

Read the story of Elijah in 1 Kings 17 about how God fed him with food delivered by ravens, and then by a widow who had only a handful of meal (flour). The widow's barrel of flour could not be used up because of her unlimited supply in God's storehouse. He did not supply the flour because she sought it, but because she *obeyed Him.*

The order has ever been "seek ye first the kingdom of God." That's why we *must* surrender the natural to the spiritual, and lay upon the altar the whole of our Adamic natures—so that Christ might be to us spiritually *and* physically all He has promised to be.

The order of the Lord has always been creation and then re-creation. First that which is natural and *then that which is spiritual.* In the Book of Jeremiah we read:

The word which came to Jeremiah from the LORD, saying,

Arise, and go down to the potter's house, and there I will cause thee to hear my words.

Then I went down to the potter's house, and, behold, he wrought a work on the wheels.

And the vessel that he made of clay was marred in the hand of the potter: so he made it again another vessel, as seemed good to the potter to make it.

Then the word of the LORD came to me, saying,

O house of Israel, cannot I do with you as this potter? saith the LORD. Behold, as the clay is in the potter's hand, so are ye in mine hand, O house of Israel.

(Jeremiah 18: 1-6.)

God never does a "patched-up job." The vilest sinners become "new creations" when they put themselves into His hands. (See 2 Corinthians 5:17.) The disease may be of the flesh, but the cure is of the spirit. The marred vessel must be put back into the hands of the Potter, that He might make it another vessel—one of His own choosing.

A Complete Work

Many people come for physical healing only. They want the Lord to touch their body, when often the Lord wants to touch their spirit. God is Spirit, and the flow of resurrection life needed for healing must come through the spirit and not through the physical flesh. When Jesus said, "I have come that ye might have life and that ye might have it more abundantly," He spoke not only of eternal life, but of His resurrection life that would permeate every atom of our beings and saturate us with its glory.

Many come looking for healing but not for the healer. Their prayers may have seemed to no avail, but no petition can ever be offered in vain, and unanswered prayer today does not necessarily mean it will be unanswered tomorrow. "Beloved, I wish above all things that thou mayest prosper and be in health, even as thy soul prospereth" (3 John 2:1). Change externally is of necessity often superseded by change internally—transformed by His Spirit in the inner person before the manifestation of the transformation is seen in the outer person.

The Scripture from John's Epistle throws a divine light upon the subject of healing. *Here is prosperity for the complete person.* But the prosperity and health is dependent upon the prosperity that is within the soul. That's why people who say, "If the Lord will heal me, I'll serve Him as long as I live," are 'putting the cart before the horse.' They are looking for the manifestation of His power from the *outside in,* when His power only operates from the *inside out.* The healing rays of the Lord's resurrection life don't shine *upon us from the outside*, but shine *through us from within.*

It's good when we sing, "Come To Jesus." It's better when we say, "Jesus has come to me." But it's best when we can declare, "He lives within my heart." Christians who need healing should seek out the elders and call for prayer from some consecrated man or woman, but it's not God's ultimate. In Christ we need no priest, for He is our "high priest" (Hebrews 4:14). In Him we need no intermediary, for He is the "one mediator between God and men" (1 Timothy 2:5).

To Him we take our whole being. We take it in consecration and surrender. We yield it to Him to do with as He will. Then we leave our vessel of clay in the hands of the Heavenly Potter, Who makes it yet another vessel after His pleasure. Though our vessel may be broken, He doesn't throw it away—with tenderness and love He reshapes us, and imparts Himself to us as our healing in body, soul, and spirit.

Examining the Cause

There's a verse that we don't like to apply to ourselves, but only to Jesus: "Though he were a Son, yet learned he obedience by the things which he suffered" (Hebrews 5:8). If that was true of our Lord, the sinless Son of God, is it possible that sometimes our suffering comes to teach us obedience? If that's possible, shouldn't we seek our Healer rather than our healing so that we may learn the cause of our suffering? Because we tend to deal with the effects, we constantly look upon and pray for them, but it's more pleasing to our Father to ask for grace to examine the cause. That's why *what we are is far more important than what we do.*

When We Stop, He Starts

We read about faith that will move mountains, and immediately begin to look at the mountains instead of seeking the faith that will move them. Jesus is the author and the finisher of our faith—so if faith begins and ends in Him, why should we struggle to manufacture it, when He alone can impart it? How sweet is His lovely presence, and how beyond description is the exercise of *His faith* and the manifestation of *His power*. In ourselves, we can do nothing—*absolutely nothing!*

We get so cluttered attending to external details, and so weary in our unceasing toil, that we fail to hear Jesus' voice say, "Come unto Me and rest. Lay down, thou weary soul, lay down, Thy head upon My breast." It's when we do that we discover it's not our faith in Him, but *His faith operating in us.* Healing doesn't come by the might of our prayers, nor by the powerful thundering of our entreaties, but by the beautiful moving of His Spirit. A woman who had been healed in body, soul, and spirit, and who was a living miracle of the recreative power of our Lord, said, "It was when I stopped that Jesus started!"

We are closest to healing when we come to the place where we say, "I cannot, but *He can!*"

12

Living Waters

When Jesus was born, there was no room for him in the inn—because all the rooms were occupied. There's a spiritual lesson for us in that. The inspired Apostle Paul wrote:

> I bow my knees unto the Father of our Lord Jesus Christ,
>
> Of whom the whole family in heaven and earth is named,
>
> That he would grant you, according to the riches of his glory, to be strengthened with might by his Spirit in the inner man;
>
> That Christ may dwell in your hearts by faith . . .
>
> (Ephesians 3:14-17)

If we have the faith, and the willingness, Christ will dynamically indwell our hearts, and from there rule and guide our lives. He will be our inner strength and the light of our lives. But when He comes, He will not—indeed, cannot—enter if He finds the rooms of our hearts are occupied and there is no place within to take up His abiding.

If only we realized that His coming will bring life, light, and health, we wouldn't be so preoccupied with giving place to our selfish, fleshly desires and purposes that crowd Him out. He who bore our sicknesses and sorrows wants to abide in our hearts to give us His peace, rest, and joy.

Jesus said, "When the Son of man cometh, shall he find faith on the earth?" (Luke 18:8). Let's take that one step further—will He find faith *in* the earth, in these bodies of clay we inhabit? If we were less concerned about what we do, would forget our petty bickering about Scripture interpretations, and open our hearts wide to let Christ in, we would return to the power and glory of the early Church. All heaven would rejoice in such a surrender as that.

Do you believe Him enough to make room for Him?

From the Inside Out

Christ doesn't come as a postman bringing gifts from the Father and leaving them at our door and then walking away. Some people use the Bible like a mail-order catalog. They ask the Father to give them what they want, and then expect the angelic messengers to bring it to them so their own desires might be gratified, and their needs met in the way they want them to be. But the light that Christ brings doesn't shine from the outside in, it radiates from the *inside out. Whatever* gifts He imparts He administers and operates. He doesn't give light, He is the light. He doesn't impart health, He is the health. *It's the constant acknowledgment of His indwelling that brings us into vital union with Him.*

Room for the incoming Christ is made within our hearts by His Spirit in accordance to the measure of our surrender and death to self. The resulting transformation may be only spiritual at first. Or it may be a feeling of peace and spiritual well-being greater than any we have known before. Whatever it is, if we have emptied the rooms of our hearts and invited Him in by faith, then He has come to abide, and from there rule and guide our lives. Following this experience of His manifested grace, the cup of His mercy will overflow and our physical body will begin to feed on His resurrection life. Instead of struggle, it is peace. Instead of agonizing, it is resting. The consciousness that Christ is dwelling within, and that He has taken the government of our lives upon His own shoulders, brings us into a blessed quietness as we hear Him say, "Be still and know that I am God."

The Great Physician

When sickness visits homes, many call for a physician who comes to the house and diagnoses the case. The first thing the doctor does is to find out, if he can, what the difficulty is. When he arrives at his conclusion, he prescribes the remedy. It's the remedy for which the patient waits. The doctor is only a means to the remedy. He takes out a little pad of blanks, writes down a prescription, and someone goes to the drugstore to return with some pills—or whatever the prescribed remedy might be. The confidence of the patient is in the remedy. The sufferer looks for the healing to be in the pills. The faith and trust the patient places in the doctor goes only so far as to hope that he knows the remedy, and that he knows what he's doing when he writes the prescription. When the pill is taken, however, the patient settles back and waits for the pill to do its work.

How different it is with the Lord Jesus. The virtue is not in what He prescribes, or in doing this or in doing that. It's not even in knowing "how to receive healing." The virtue is in the person of the Lord Jesus Christ. He sees us in our sick and sinful state of impurity, and He knows that the only remedy is holiness. We have read that, too, and have made the mistake of struggling to become holy. There is no such thing as holiness apart from Him. Holiness is not something He gives us, holiness is what He is. *What Christ has is what He is—what He gives is what He is.*

Some go to the altar and pray for sanctification and sometimes jump to their feet and say, "Praise the Lord, the work is done." But Christ doesn't give sanctification to anyone. *He is our sanctification!* When His life overflows our lives, we are truly sanctified in Him. "But of Him are ye in Christ Jesus, who of God is made unto us wisdom, and righteousness, and sanctification, and redemption: that, according as it is written, He that glorieth, let him glory in the Lord" (1 Corinthians 1:30-31).

It's the same in divine healing. We don't prescribe pills or tell the sick person, "Now you must do this, and you must do that, and then the Lord will touch you with healing power." It's not a question of being made right in our own righteousness, or ready with our own readiness, for in James 5:15 we read, "and if he have committed sins, they shall be forgiven him." What the poor, broken, sufferers need—in all their unworthiness, and even in their sin—is to come to the Lord in absolute surrender and let Him into their hearts.

The Way to Victory

This is the reason then that there *must* be death to self. There *must* be acknowledgment of His Lordship and Headship. He must be Savior *to* us, and Lord *over* us. It *must* be His will alone and not ours, and not a mixture of His will and ours. Beneath the outstretched arms of the trees in the Garden, our

Lord cried, *"If* it be possible, let this cup pass from Me." Then He complete abandoned Himself to God and to the purpose and will of His Father, and finished, "Nevertheless, not My will but Thine be done." The only way to the Resurrection was through the Garden, and through the Garden to the Cross—and He has to bring us the same way and to the same place. "Because I live" He said, "Ye too shall live." But *His* resurrection life in us must be preceded by *our* death. Even the seemingly good side of our Adamic nature has to go to the Cross with the acknowledged bad. As it was in the days of old, so it is still today: "Slay utterly" all that is an abomination to God, "and all our righteousness are as filthy rags" (Isaiah 64:6). Christ has been made unto us righteousness, and His righteous life alone must be all that lives in us and through us. (See 1 Corinthians 1:30.) This is our only way to victory— there is no other.

The Living Way

In the days of Jesus' earthly walk, the Pharisees cried, "Lo, here is truth!" and the Sadducees, in contradiction, said, "No, it is here." Grecian philosophers had long proclaimed that they had the truth. Our Blessed Lord, however, silenced them all in His declaration, "I am the way, the truth, and the life. No man cometh unto the Father but by Me." There is no difference today. He is our way. He is our truth. He is our life. There is no other way. There is no other truth. There is no other life. The way, the truth, and the life dwells in us, but how much of Him is dynamically active in us is directly dependent upon how much of ourselves we have surrendered to Him.

It may hurt a bit to surrender completely, but the Spirit of truth must bring us to that point before the Lord of glory can indwell our often fickle hearts, which must be fickle and wavering no more.

97

Under testing, a woman cried, "I cannot bear this cross!" The voice divine responded, "Do you want Me to take this cross away?" But before she could answer, her understanding was supernaturally quickened; and it was revealed that if it were removed, a harder cross—one to which she was not accustomed—might be substituted. So she did not ask for its removal. In a short time, however, the same spoke again, "Now, commit it unto me." With the commitment came a glorious light of revelation that God Himself was raising to take action. Beneath the cross of her burden, the everlasting arms lifted the load from her, and through her surged resurrection life and turned her cross into a crown.

What a privilege and joy it is to surrender! How blessed it is to be invited to lay our all at the Master's feet. How poor is our understanding in comparison with His. How faulty our Adamic wills are in the light of the divine will that was fulfilled in Christ. Beloved, there can be no shortcuts. The inspired Word declares that if anyone try to climb up any other way, the same is a thief and a robber, for the Lord Jesus Christ is the only door to God. No man can come to the Father but by Him. How sweet it is to reminisce as well as testify,

> I've found a Friend, oh, such a Friend!
> He loved me e'er I knew Him!
> He drew me with the chords of love,
> And thus He bound me to Him!

We love to speak doctrinally about the Father seeing us in Christ, but to my heart is whispered the truth that He would first see *Christ in us.*

13

The Living Word

Before Jesus was born, God's people had only the spoken and written Word. God revealed His thoughts in various ways to a chosen few and inspired them to write the Scriptures so that others could read and walk by the light of His written Word. Then the day came when "the Word was made flesh, and dwelt among us" (John 1:14).

In the King James Version, quoted above, it says that "the Word was *made* flesh," but it should read—as later translations do—"the Word *became* flesh." The word "made" denotes something new, something that did not exist before, and was therefore produced or manufactured. But the eternal Word pre-existed with God and was God, and came to earth not as something new, something made, but in a new manifestation. The Word "became" flesh—that is, was tabernacled in a human body.

As the written Word was the *thought* of God, so the Living Word became the *embodiment of that thought*, the thought personified in the person of our Lord Jesus.

That's why every statement He spoke was impregnated with this truth: "I am come that they might have life, and that they might have it more abundantly" (John 10:10). The words He spoke were spirit and they were life. He "was the true Light, which lighteth every man that cometh into the world" (John 1:9), for "God is light, and in Him is no darkness at all" (I John 1:5), and those who follow Him shall not walk in darkness, but shall have the light of life.

Christ is our Life. He is our Healing. He is our strength. Not the word of the printed page, not our faulty interpretations of that written word, but the Word made flesh—the Living Word. The Word of God that once dwelt among us, is now the Living Word who dwells within us. He was the personification of the Word of God, the Word of God living and moving among people. And we can become that, also, for by His life in us we are changed from glory to glory into His image.

Many have taken a few of His sentences and built marvelous sermons around them. He has become an ideal example to imitate, someone to pattern our lives and conduct after. Now that is all very well as far as it goes, but it certainly misses the mark of the high calling of God in Christ Jesus. What He said was a divine revelation of what He is. The things that He said and did were only the outward manifestations, the effulgent glory, of what He Himself was.

Paul didn't cry for wisdom to know more *about* Him. From the hungry depths of his innermost being, he cried, "I count all things but loss . . . that I may *know* Him, and the power of His resurrection!" It's this *vital union* with Christ that is necessary in our lives. We must stop our struggling to become like Him, stop trying to imitate Him. There's no need to spent long hours reading the biography of a king when you're in his royal presence.

He is Our Life

The promises concerning Jesus include not only what He would do, but also what He would be. The miracle of His grace is not merely what He would do for us, but what He would become *in us*. It would have been wonderful, indeed, had He come to show us a plan whereby we could find salvation, but it is unspeakably precious when we realize *He died to become that salvation.* Could a man receive salvation and refuse the Savior? Is there such a thing as Christianity without Christ? Could one ever be spiritual, without the Spirit? That's why our ecclesiastical rituals avail us nothing. Too many have made them substitutes for His lovely, indwelling presence, and have tried to find sanctuary for their wounded spirits within the ceremony. By so doing, they have often stopped the King of Glory from entering into their hearts.

One truth that stands out in bold relief in the ministry and life of our Lord, is the privilege of progression and growth in grace and in the knowledge of the things of God. The Apostle Paul proclaimed this same glorious truth, and admonished us to go on to maturity. That maturity is the unhindered outflow of the knowledge of Christ Himself, giving us understanding of the heart according to our spiritual ability to receive Him.

The growth of the Christian life is, in reality, the increasing manifestation of His life. "He that believeth in (into) Me, out of his innermost being shall flow rivers of Living Water." The outpouring of this divine flow of resurrection life will cover body, soul, and spirit—and the divine virtues of our Lord will nullify and abrogate absolutely everything we have received under the curse of the Law. This provision includes healing. It means more than healing, it means the perpetuation of health. It means the continuous operation in us of the resurrected life of Christ.

Christ is All

Oh that the sheep of His pasture, so cruelly beaten about by the forces of circumstance and environment, could once again hear the voice of the Good Shepherd, saying, "Come unto Me!" What an innumerable host of cults surround us, and with what insistence they proclaim their dogmatisms and their private interpretations. Divine healers shamelessly promote their wares, merchandising this method or that method for a gift-offering of any size, and measuring out the atoning sacrifice of our Lord as if it were sunlight you can sell by the bottleful.

In the days of old, the Pharisees and Sadducees placed every kind of demand upon the people before they would be accepted by the various religious leaders. They were required to give tithes where it could be proved that they had given. They must pray in public. They must do this and they must not do that. With legalisms they bound them and with chains of ritualism they enslaved them. But when Jesus came, He swept aside their traditional beliefs. He upset the apple-cart of their preconceived and pre-established prejudices. He showed His disdain for their Sabbath laws and healed people for no other reason than that they needed His touch, no matter the day or the way. His tender appeal was directed to the hearts and spirits of the suffering, the sinful, and the oppressed.

"Come unto Me!" He said. That was all. They had only to come close enough for His touch. There was no need to go through this gate or that door, for there was only *one* door after Jesus came. There was only *one* way. There was only *one* life. There was only *one* salvation. *It was all in the Savior!* They came directly to Him, and there flowed into them from Him—from His unlimited fountain of virtue—life, health, strength, joy, and peace. He was their Everything! They needed nothing beside Him. Whether it was a self-righteous

Nicodemus, a blind Bartimaeus, or a demon oppressed Mary Magdalene, He was the unlimited source of God's grace, and in Him they found all that they needed.

How intellectual we've tried to be, how complicated we've made it, and how simple it really is. Whatever our problems, all we need do is determine within our hearts that no matter what others say or tell us to do, we will ourselves touch Jesus. Then like the woman with the issue of blood who pressed through the throng to the side of her Lord, we must push aside people with their jargon of contending voices, and crowd our way through every beckoning group until we stand face to face with eternal peace—our Lord Jesus Christ Himself. The sunlight from His lovely face will warm our hearts, and the doors of our Spirits will open wide to let "the light of life" stream in!

As Many as Received

He says, "Give Me your poor, broken, wasted life, and in return I will give you Mine. Give Me your weakness—battered and bruised by man's inhumanity to man and the cruelty of sinful circumstance—give it to Me, and I will give you My courage, My strength, and power. I died that you might live; and now as you die to all that is self, I live in you. I surrendered to the will of God for you; and now you *must* surrender—*absolutely and completely*—to the will of the Father through Me."

We left God in disobedience (in Adam all die) and we return in obedience (in Christ all are made alive). In Christ we come back into the direct care and keeping of our Creator. In God's glorious eternal heaven there will be no need of the sun, neither of the moon, for the Lamb Himself is the Light thereof. The light that illumines heaven is the light that illumines our spirits—and through our spirits our souls and bodies. *In this life we should not be seeking the limelight—we should be seeking the Lamb-light.*

In the final analysis, we can throw out—or otherwise push aside—most of the things we have been taught to do—do—do! Why strive to light our little candles when the sun is brightly shining? Why try we to push the ocean back, when our heavenly Father has ordained that the force of gravity and the pull of the moon shall do that with consummate ease? It's God's will that His sheep not wander about in blind superstition, seeking first this and then that as a source of healing. It's His desire that each of His children come into direct contact, and live in union with Christ, that all may come to the Father through Him.

Yet—how pitiful appears the account! He came unto His own and His own received Him not. He was the light that shone in darkness, and the darkness understood it not. He was the fulfillment of every prophetic utterance, and yet the students of the prophecies did not recognize Him. He called to people in need, but they turned deaf ears to Him and followed after superstitions and fables. In their blind ignorance and superstition they knew not what He said, let alone what He meant. He spoke of the bread of heaven that He was, and all they could think about was the manna that fell from heaven on the burning sands of the wilderness centuries before. He spoke of rivers of living water that He would be, but they could visualize nothing beyond the pouring of some water from a pool upon a pile of stones they called an altar. Like today, they would believe anything, do anything, except simply receive Him!

Why was that so then, why is it so now?

Because receiving Him means giving up to Him the right to one's self!

But how much is missed, for the heart that opens to the reign of Christ enters into the reality of His Presence. It is, as it were, that in the heart the lion and the lamb lie down together. We walk with Him in heavenly places. He speaks, and the sound of His voice is so sweet that the winds hush their noise, and the storms quiet down to listen. The living, pulsating reality of His divine indwelling springs up within our innermost being like an artesian well of heavenly glory. It is effortless. The river of His life just flows until it permeates every fiber of our nature—and we don't have to wait until the gates of pearl unfold to be lost in wonder, love, and praise.

As the human spirit runs up the flag of unconditional surrender, the flesh capitulates, and the Lord of life is sovereign. Christ is all, and in all—and throughout our being all that Christ was, He now becomes in us. We drink of His life, His healing, His saving grace, and His strength. His perfect love casts out all fear, and we learn to know Him as the only wise God, the true mediator between God and us, the man Christ Jesus.

If, perchance, the trials of the road become heavy, we learn to find our sufficiency not in human attainment, but in that faith—the faith of the Lord Jesus Christ—which worketh by love; and which will surmount every difficulty, be it physical, material, or spiritual. This all-sufficiency can be found only in the outworking of the indwelling Christ, for it is in Him and through Him that all our needs are met.

Section II

Healing

Preface to Section II

One of the greatest healings that ever took place through Dr. Price's ministry was that of the sister of Demos Shakarian, the founder of Full Gospel Business Men's Fellowship International.

One early morning in Downey, California, Shakarian's sister, Florence, failed to see a stop sign because of a thick fog and ran into a road repair truck, spilling tons of boiling tar onto the road. The impact threw Florence from her car and rolled her through the tar, crushing her left hip and pelvis and burning her back severely.

In the hospital's intensive care unit, the deep burns prevented the doctors from setting the broken bones, and within a few days a series of x-rays showed fragments of splintered bones traveling toward vital organs in her abdomen. Shakarian's church held a twenty-four hour fast for her healing as he headed for the town of Maywood, just five miles from Downey, where he had heard that Dr. Price was holding a tent meeting.

When he got there, he had to park his car over half a mile from the tent because of the crowd and walk the rest of the way. Inside the huge tent there was standing room only. Dr. Price was still speaking. When he finished his sermon, he invited all those in need of healing to come forward. Hundreds went, and he prayed over each of them and anointed them with oil. Shakarian kept looking at this watch. It was 9 P.M. when Dr. Price started praying, and after 11 P.M. before he finished. The ushers kept trying to close the meeting by telling the people that Dr. Price would be there the next day to pray for the sick, but few listened to them.

Finally the last one was prayed for, and Dr. Price started gathering up His Bible and bottle of oil. Shakarian called out, "Sir!"

Dr. Price looked up to see who was speaking, and Shakarian dodged past an usher to get to him and exclaimed in one breath, "Dr. Price, my name is Demos Shakarian and my sister's been in an automobile accident and the doctors say she can't live and we wondered if you'd come."

Dr. Price closed his eyes wearily and was silent for a moment. Then suddenly he said, "I'll come."

Shakarian hurried on ahead of him through the slowly dispersing crowd, and fretted every time someone stopped them. Dr. Price saw his impatience and said, "Don't be anxious, son, your sister will be healed tonight." Then when he saw Shakarian's puzzled expression over how he could be so certain, he explained.

In 1924, not long after his baptism in the Holy Spirit in Aimee Semple McPherson's meeting, he was traveling through Canada and came to the small town of Paris, Ontario. As he drove through the town, he felt strange urgings to turn one way and then another until he found himself in front of a Methodist church, where he now felt he should stop. Without knowing why he was doing it, he went to the parsonage next door, introduced himself as an evangelist, and asked if he could hold a series of meetings in the church. The pastor looked almost as surprised as Dr. Price felt when he said, "Yes."

Among those attending the meeting was Eva Johnson, whose letter to Dr. Price you read in the first chapter of this book, and her husband, Louis. Ten years before, Eva had an attack of rheumatic fever that left her in constant pain and unable to walk or care for herself. During the years her legs twisted and shriveled, and the right one drew up behind the left one and froze in that position. Over the years, twenty different doctors had treated her, but like the woman with the issue of blood her condition only grew worse.

Night after night she came to the meetings and nothing happened, and then one night Dr. Price *knew* that Eva was going to be healed during the meeting. The reason he was certain was that each time he looked at her a tangible physical warmth settled across his shoulders. He interpreted that sensation as being the presence of Christ. The rest of the story is told in chapter one of the Real Faith section.

"And tonight, when you spoke to me," Dr. Price continued, "that warmth fell upon my shoulders again. It's there now. Christ is in this situation, and your sister will be healed."

It was almost midnight when they reached the hospital and entered Florence's room. Barely conscious, she lay in a bed of salve amidst an array of tubes and wires strung through pulleys. Heavy traction weights were suspended from the ends of the wires. Florence nodded weakly when Demos introduced Dr. Price to her.

Dr. Price poured a bit of anointing oil from his bottle into his hand, reached through the tubes and wires surrounding her, and touched his fingertips to her forehead. "Lord Jesus," he prayed, "we thank You for being here. We thank You for healing our sister." Demos later testified that at that moment the room's atmosphere changed somehow—the air became thicker, almost as if they were surrounded by water.

Then one of the traction weights swung toward Dr. Price and he jumped back as it went past his head. This was followed by all the weights beginning to swing wildly back and forth. Florence rolled from side to side on her bed as the weights swung. Though Demos knew his sister should be kept immobile, he seemed wrapped and bathed in pulsating air and unable to be concerned over what was happening to his sister, who was now groaning from either pain or ecstasy.

For twenty minutes the weights kept swinging, and though the nurses were scheduled to check on Florence every ten minutes, no one entered the room. There was just Florence, Demos, Dr. Price, and the Nameless Presence that filled the room with warmth. Then, just as suddenly as they started, the weights stopped swinging and slowly came to a stop—and they were just three people in a normal hospital room.

Florence looked up at her brother and whispered, "Demos, Jesus healed me."

He bent over her, "I know," he said.

A few minutes later, when the nurse came in, Florence was sound asleep.

Demos drove Dr. Price to his home in Pasadena, and returned to his own home in Downey. He was still asleep when Florence's doctor called, his voice breaking with excitement. "Demos, you've got to come down and look at these x-rays."

When he got to the hospital, he found the x-ray room jammed with every doctor, nurse, and technician that could crowd into it. On the light screens on the wall were eight x-ray negatives. Seven showed Florence's crushed left hip and pelvis, and bone fragments gradually moving toward her vital organs. The eighth negative showed a pelvis and hip that were totally normal, with only a few thin lines that indicated that once there had been injuries—and no bone fragments anywhere. The x-ray had been taken that morning.

Strangely, the burns on Florence's back weren't healed, and she remained in the hospital for another month until her back had healed enough for her to leave. A few days later, she told Demos that the night before she left the hospital, she had a dream in which twenty-five glasses of water were placed on a table for her to drink. "I believe the dream means that God has given me twenty-five more years in which to serve Him," she said.

Twenty-five years later Florence died.

1

Scriptural Basis for Healing

Two questions naturally come to mind when thinking about divine healing:

1. What scriptural authority is there for people praying for the sick?

2. What does the Bible teach about divine healing methods?"

These questions are natural because if we have no scriptural authority we should never pray for the sick, and if there is no clear Bible teaching on the question of our healing we should never claim it. The Word of God is a lamp unto our feet and a light unto our path. When we go outside the Word for our experiences, we inevitably enter into darkness and stumble along unscriptural paths. But if it's in the Word we should claim it and appropriate it unto ourselves and give glory to God. Why claim part of the promises and let the rest go by? Why be satisfied with a partial gospel when the Bible teaches us there's a wonderful full gospel that includes provisions for the spirit, soul, *and* body?

Here are some of the Scriptures that pertain to healing and the wonderful provisions that God has made for healing and health for the whole person. As always in the Scriptures, some of the provisions require that certain conditions be met before the promise will be manifested.

God's covenant of healing with His people: Exodus 15:26; Numbers 21:8-9.

Blessings of obedience: Deuteronomy 28:1-14.

God's healing Word: Psalm 107:17-21; Proverbs 4:20-22.

God's will is to heal His children: Matthew 8:1-17; Mark 1:41; Luke 5:13;

God's will is for His children to be healthy and live long: Exodus 23:25; Proverbs 4:10; Ephesians 6:2-3; 3 John 1:2.

Healing in the Atonement: Psalm 103:3; Isaiah 53:4-5; Matthew 8:17.

The Children's bread and their right: Matthew 15:22-28; Mark 7:25-30.

Christ's testimony of Himself: Luke 4:16-21, 7:19-23.

Peter's testimony of Christ: Acts 10:38.

Christ's commission to His Church: Mark 16:14-20; Luke 9:1-2, 10:1-9.

Healing provision for the Church: James 5:14-16.

Power of faith: Matthew 9:29, 17:20, Mark 9:23, 11:11-23; John 14:12; Acts 14:9.

Believing prayer: Matthew 21:22; Mark 11:24; John 14:13-14, 16:23-24; 1 John 3:22.

In the book of Exodus is the story of God delivering the Israelites from Egypt and making a covenant of healing with them. Moses had brought the Israelites from the Red Sea into the wilderness of Shur, and they went three days and found no water. Then the cloud led them to Marah, but the water there was bitter, and so, naturally, they murmured against Moses, saying, "What shall we drink?" (Exodus 15:24). Moses had no answer and so he did what we should all do in an impossible situation, "he cried unto the LORD."

In response to Moses' cry, "the LORD showed him a tree, which when he had cast into the waters, the waters were made sweet" (Exodus 15:25). The LORD then "made for them a statute and an ordinance, and there he proved [tested] them." He said:

If thou wilt diligently hearken to the voice of the LORD thy God, and wilt do that which is right in his sight, and wilt give ear to his commandments, and keep all his statutes, I will put none of these diseases upon

115

thee, which I have brought upon the Egyptians: for I am the LORD that healeth thee.

(Exodus 15:26)

This promise of healing was given to a wayward people. It was given to a people who would meet that opening word, "If," face to face and measure up to the standard of obedience that God demanded. And whenever they measured up God fulfilled the promise. But here we can clearly see the relationship between obedience and divine healing.

Some years later leprosy came upon Miriam, the sister of Moses, because of the sin of backbiting and criticizing her brother. Sin and sickness took hold upon her together and there was no bodily healing for her until atonement for sin had been made. As he always did, "Moses cried unto the LORD, saying, Heal her now, O God, I beseech thee" (1 Numbers 12:13). God heard his cry, and Miriam was delivered from leprosy after the atonement for her sin that the LORD demanded. (See verse 14.) So it has always been. The promises for healing are not to a wicked generation, but to those who have received Christ, and, knowing His power to save, are convinced of His might to heal.

Divine healing runs throughout all of the Old Testament and on into the New Testament. The promises are written eternally in heaven and are fulfilled in every age for those who are in Christ Jesus. Isaiah the prophet foresaw it and wrote:

Surely he hath borne our griefs, and carried our sorrows: yet we did esteem him stricken, smitten of God, and afflicted.

But he was wounded for our transgressions, he was bruised for our iniquities: the chastisement of our peace was upon him; and with his stripes we are healed.

(Isaiah 53:4-5)

Now some have objected and said that the healing referred to in Isaiah is the healing of the soul and is spiritual, and has no relation to healing for the body. That objection is easily answered by the Scriptures themselves. Chapter 8 of the Book of Matthew is filled with healings performed by the Lord—He healed a leper, a Centurion's servant, Peter's mother, and then "When the even was come, they brought unto him many that were possessed with devils: and he cast out the spirits with his word, and healed all that were sick" (Matthew 8:16).

God heals because of His grace and compassion, but there was another reason why Jesus was healing on that day. It was to fulfill that which was spoken about Him by Isaiah—and in stating that through Matthew, the Holy Spirit Himself gave us the true interpretation of Isaiah's words: "Himself took our infirmities, and bare our sicknesses." If the Holy Spirit interprets Isaiah's words as meaning physical healing, who dare say that they refer only to spiritual healing of the soul? It would take a foolish person, indeed, to contradict the Holy Spirit!

To any unprejudiced reader of the Scriptures, it's clear as the noonday sun that at the whipping post Jesus provided for all the healing any child of God would ever need. Even prior to that the Lord gave power to the twelve and then to seventy more and sent them forth with specific instructions to preach the gospel and heal the sick. The good news of salvation for the soul and healing for the body was carried wherever they went to whoever would hear. It has been the same ever since then. It was so under the Old Covenant and it is still so under the better New Covenant!

Prior to Pentecost the disciples taught and healed with the Master, and when the Lord said His last good-bye and ascended from Olivet, they went into Jerusalem to tarry for the enduement with power that He said they would receive. On the day of Pentecost it came in blazing glory, and from that upper room they marched forth as tongues of living fire. Baptized with the Holy Ghost, filled with the glory of the Lord, preaching, teaching and proclaiming the kingdom of a resurrected Christ, the apostles went from city to city and healed the sick wherever they found them.

Eight years later they were still doing it, and were now joined by ordinary Church people—table waiters. One of them, Philip, went to Samaria and started holding meetings, so they called him an evangelist. Philip not only preached the gospel of Jesus Christ, he also healed the sick, just as Jesus had told His disciples to do. Far and wide the apostles and disciples took the good news of the saving, healing, Christ, "the Lord working with them, and confirming the word with signs following. Amen" (Mark 16:20).

Now some have said that the gift of healing was given to the disciples to enable them to establish the Christian Church, and at the end of the 'Apostolic period' the gifts were taken from the Church. All such objectors should be asked one question: "Would you please give me the chapter and verse where it says that?" As an answer, you generally will get a long system of explanation in which no direct Scripture verses are given, and in which verses like the ones in the fifth chapter of James are entirely ignored.

James was the chairman of the first meeting held by the Church leaders. He was austere, conservative, dignified, and well versed in the Scriptures—he was also the Lord's brother. In addition, he would have received counsel in Church matters from the apostles themselves.

He was, therefore, eminently qualified to know the mind of the Lord, to follow the guidance of the Holy Spirit, and to give instructions to the dispersed disciples about how they should act and what they should do. It is important that we realize this, for in the last chapter of his Epistle "to the twelve tribes which are scattered abroad," he writes this about healing:

Is any among you afflicted? let him pray. Is any merry? let him sing psalms.

Is any sick among you? let him call for the elders of the church; and let them pray over him, anointing him with oil in the name of the Lord:

And the prayer of faith shall save the sick, and the Lord shall raise him up; and if he have committed sins, they shall be forgiven him.

Confess your faults one to another, and pray one for another, that ye may be healed. The effectual fervent prayer of a righteous man availeth much.

(James 5:13-16)

If anyone has the right to single out that passage and claim without direct scriptural authority that those verses applied *only* to Apostolic times or the kingdom age, then another person has the same right to make the same claim for the whole Epistle. But, praise be to the Lord!—thousands of people all over the country can testify to the fact that Jesus Christ is "the same yesterday, and today, and forever" (Hebrews 13:8), and that He has not only the power to save, but the power to heal. Beloved, if you need healing, pray through every fog and mist of doubt and unbelief until the promises of God are made real to you, and the healing grace and faith of Christ overshadow you.

The limitations of God's power are the limitations of our own faith. Provision has been made for physical healing, and the people whose spiritual eyes have been opened can see for certain that there is ample scriptural authority for praying for the sick. If there was no direct or indirect reference to the physical body, we still have a multitude of promises upon which to stand in asking for the physical restoration of ourselves or others. Explore the Scriptures that I've listed and you will see this for yourself.

A Young Girl is Healed

Everywhere in the filled arena the Christians lifted their hearts and voices together in prayer for the sick and disabled. The platform was crowded with rows of people who needed the touch of a healing Christ. The other ministers and I prayed for the older folks first and anointed them with oil. Some of them crossed the stage with their hands lifted toward heaven and their bodies shaking as they sobbed with gratitude because they had felt His presence.

About mid-way through the prayer line, a little girl stood in front of me. She had tears in her eyes as she looked up at me, and I could see her lips moving in prayer. I knelt by her side, and asked, "Darling, what is it you want of the Lord?"

She looked shyly at me for a moment and then said, "I want Jesus to heal me, if you please."

"What's your trouble, my dear?" I asked.

For an answer she put forward one of her little limbs, and I saw that she wore steel braces around both legs—legs that were wasted and too weak for her to stand without support. She then took hold of one of my hands and moved it around to her back, and there I discovered that her back and shoulders were encased in a network of steel and straps. She had that dreaded disease, *polio*. With a trembling little voice she told me that some of the straps never came off—not even at night after her prayers when she laid down to sleep.

I hugged her for a moment in silent prayer, and then asked, "Tell me, little sister, do you believe that Jesus will heal you?"

Faster than I can write this she answered, "Oh, I just know He will, because in the Bible He promised to heal us and Mamma says He just loves little children."

Now if I was a skeptic or a critic or an unbelieving believer, I *might* have taken her in my arms and said:

No, dear, you're mistaken. Jesus won't heal you. He used to heal little children long ago when He was on earth. He *used* to make little paralyzed limbs whole again so that little girls like you could run and laugh and play. But He doesn't anymore. You see, my poor little girl, he did it in the old days by the waters of Galilee and the cities of old Judea because he wanted to prove He really was the Son of God. And later, dear, He let His disciples pray for little girls like you so He could start His Church. But once it got started, He took all the power away. No, dear, you must go along and make the best of it. I know there's no hope for you, that no human physician can help you, and the Great Physician *doesn't* help little girls like you anymore. What's that? About the Bible promises? Well now, some day you'll understand. You see, the Bible talks about healing and praying for the sick, but it doesn't really mean it. It did mean it once, and some great theologians say it might mean it again—but it doesn't mean it for you today—or tomorrow. Hobble along there, now, dear. Make the best of it. Dry those little eyes and some day, perhaps—someday—you might . . . but you probably won't.

No! No! No! I cannot tell her that! On the pulpit near me is the Word. The Word of the Lion of the tribe of Judah. The word of the Omnipotent God. The Word that speaks of authority and power. The Word of truth. The Word of our Lord and Master. So instead I prayed, and as I did I felt a presence by my side—I couldn't see Him, couldn't hear His voice, but He was there—I knew Him, and I could feel Him.

"Jesus, Savior, Healer, Lord, Thou didst heal people in the days of the long ago. We have read Lord how the mothers of Salem brought their children to Jesus, and we come to Thee, dear Lord, to ask Thee to lay Thine

121

own nail-pierced hand in love and healing power on the body of this little child. Heal her now, Lord."

My prayer ended in a sob as I placed on her little forehead the anointing oil and commanded the paralysis to depart in the name of the Lord Jesus Christ of Nazareth. A slight quiver went through her body. She fell backwards and laid prostrate under the power. A moment or two later I heard her saying, "Jesus, I do love you. You have healed me, Jesus. Thank you, Jesus—oh, thank you—I love you, Jesus, I love you" As she was raised to her feet totally healed and had her braces removed, the thousands who were there shouted the praises of the Lord. Across every mind and heart there seemed to be emblazoned in letters of red, "Jesus Christ the same yesterday, and today, and forever" (Hebrews 13:8).

Hundreds of men and women crowded to the altar crying out for salvation. The mother of the girl that been healed suddenly lifted her voice to heaven, and from a heart filled with love and gratitude, started to sing, "It is just like Jesus." The audience picked up the refrain and it rolled like a great organ through the building:

> It's just like Jesus to roll the clouds away,
> It's just like Jesus to keep me day by day,
> It's just like Jesus all along the way,
> It's just like His great love.

2

How to Receive Your Healing

It has been clearly shown that your healing has been provided for and that we are keeping within the bounds of good Scripture teaching when we pray for the sick and ask the Lord to touch the bodies of the sick and disabled. No one doubts that the salvation of the soul of every sin-sick seed of Adam was purchased by the Lord Jesus on Calvary, and the complete work of atonement finished there. Yet most people are still unsaved and don't know the peace of their sins forgiven. The reason is simple—they've never availed themselves of the privilege of receiving Christ as their Lord and Savior. His sacrifice on Calvary only means something to the person who believes in Him and what He did for them when He shed His blood as the Lamb of God sacrificed for the sins of the world.

So it is with physical healing. His stripes purchased our healing—in every atom of His torn flesh and splattered blood there was sufficient healing for all of our infirmities and pains. Isaiah looking forward to that scourging wrote, "with his stripes we *are* healed" (Isaiah 53:5)—while Peter looking back at that same scourging wrote, "by whose stripes ye *were* healed" (1 Peter 2:24). Whatever our ailment, our healing was accomplished two-thousand years ago at a whipping post in Jerusalem. But it isn't sufficient to simply know it, or even believe it and ask for healing. *The work is done when we accept it as done.* The Master Himself told us, "What things soever ye desire, when ye pray, believe that ye receive them, and ye shall have them" (Mark 11:14). The Greek New Testament reads this way: "Therefore I tell you, all things which ye pray and ask, believe that ye received, and it will be to you." When do you believe that you received it—*when you prayed!*

Possessing Then Feeling

Some time ago in one of the great campaigns that brought salvation and healing to thousands of people, a poor man was kneeling at the altar weeping as if his heart would break. Although there's always something that touches the heart-strings at the sight of a weeping penitent at the mourners' bench, this man especially attracted my attention because it was the fifth or sixth time he had been there. I pressed through the crowd around the altar and knelt beside him and asked if he needed help. He turned his tear-filled eyes toward me and said:

"Do I need help? I should say I do. Brother, why won't Jesus save me when He saves everybody else around here? That fellow over there just got through hollering for joy and the Lord just walks right by me. I can't get saved at all, brother, and I wish you would tell the Lord about me."

"Of course I will," I replied, "but, brother, the reason the Lord doesn't save you, is because you won't let Him. Now let me explain what I mean. I know what you're after, you're seeking for feeling. You want an experience like these other people around here who have testified and been shouting the praises of the Lord. I don't blame you for that, but you must know that you cannot feel anything you don't possess. There must be a point of contact somewhere if you're going to feel anything. I have a pencil in my hand. Can you feel it? No! Tell me why you cannot feel it. Of course, because you don't have it to feel. I feel it because I have it. Now, brother, listen to me. *How in the world can you expect to feel salvation if you don't have it? How can you feel Christ if you don't possess Him?* Remember, Jesus died to save you. He's done all He can for your redemption. Now let's pray together and ask Him to receive us."

We bowed our heads and prayed. Sentence by sentence he repeated after me the words of a simple prayer of repentance in which he also promised the Lord he would always serve Him and love Him—and in the prayer, so simple that a child could have understood the words, he received Christ as his Savior.

He opened his eyes, and gazed into mine. He didn't speak but waited for me to say something, and so I said, "Praise the Lord, brother, you belong to the King."

"Am I a Christian?" he asked incredulously.

"Why, brother, you must believe His Word," I said. "Didn't you just now take Him as your Savior and didn't He promise to save you?"

"Why, He did do that very thing, didn't He," he replied as his eyes opened a little wider. He paused in thought a moment and then he burst out: "Say, I *am* a Christian, brother. Then he asked, "If I died in a minute, would I go to heaven?"

"Surely you would, brother," I told this unchurched man of the street. "He died to save you and you are saved right now."

It was interesting to watch his face as his faith took hold. The realization dawned upon him, and his eyes flashed as he repeated to himself softly and musingly, "Saved! Saved *right now*! A Christian—a real Christian right now!" Then came a veritable explosion.

The moment he really believed it, it became real to him. Doubts were swept away. Unbelief was gone. He took one deep breath and hollered, "Hip, hip, hooray—I mean glory, hallelujah. Praise the Lord."

He jumped to his feet and shouted for all he was worth. "Oh, brother, hallelujah; oh glory, glory," until I had to quiet him and ask him to be as still as possible, for other souls were praying through to salvation. I could never understand a salvation without feeling. But salvation to be felt must be possessed, and we can only possess by faith. *Even so, healing to be felt must be possessed, and we can only possess by faith.*

3

Common Mistakes

Over the years my workers and I have prayed for hundreds-of-thousands of people, and we can say to the glory of God that we've seen thousands of people healed from all manner of diseases and sicknesses. Yet even more people were turned away empty because they did not understand. In an opening healing service in a great Vancouver campaign we prayed for only twenty-five people. Scores were there who wished to be reached, but there was such an evident lack of faith in them that we told them to wait. As people who had faith were healed night after night the great throngs of people who attended regularly had their faith grow by leaps and bounds. So much so that on the closing day of that meeting, we prayed for fifteen-hundred people *individually* at a single service. As many as one hundred at a time were prostrate under the power of God, and the faith of the people seemed to roll in great waves through the Arena. According to the estimates of the owners of the building, over 250,000 people heard the word of God in that Arena in the space of three weeks. The city of Vancouver was shaken by the grace and glory of God, and testimonies of healing came in from every direction.

Now it's impossible to pray for multitudes of people like that without knowing *why* some are healed and some people are not. In this chapter I want to deal with two common mistakes, and then show clearly how to approach the Lord in asking for physical healing.

The first mistake is *believing that the person who prays for your healing has some special virtue or anointing.*

The one who prays for you isn't your healer, but just a sinner saved by grace, a brand snatched from the eternal burning, a poor halting creature of time touched by the hand of God. No person on earth is *worthy* even to pray for you, and no one should ever put anointing oil on your head who doesn't feel unworthy even to touch the hem of Jesus' garment. Get your eyes away from the evangelist, minister, or worker, and try to focus the eyes of your soul upon the blessed One whose back was scourged for your healing.

Often when people have crowded forth and asked me to lay my hands upon them, I've felt like drawing away and saying, "Not my hands, sister, but His; not my touch, brother, but the touch of a nail-pierced hand alone can bring you relief." My heart has bled as I've seen them come so weary and sad. They are often people who have given up hope, and in whose eyes hope is finding place again. Mothers with their disabled children, and men helping the disabled or blind to the altar. Scores of them, hundreds of them, sometimes thousands of them—sick and helpless, maimed and deaf and blind. I've heard them sing:

The Great Physician now is near,
The sympathizing Jesus.
He speaks the drooping heart to cheer.
Oh hear the voice of Jesus."

As I've listened, tears have flowed freely down my cheeks and in my helplessness I've cried out unto the Lord. Only Jesus can heal! Only Jesus can save! Only Jesus can hear and answer the prayers coming from broken hearts and wounded bodies.

Then my heart has thrilled as I've heard the great crowds sing—sing in the fullness of their joy, sing in the gladness of their hearts. And why shouldn't they sing? For they've received the touch of a loving hand! Their weary lives have been blessed by the Man of Galilee! Their burdens been lifted and their sorrows rolled away!

Aye, sing on, ye blessed happy pilgrims; sing on and chant your hymns of praise. Sing until the notes that leave your lips roll over the battlements of glory and lodge near a throne of alabaster white in the realms of eternal day. Sing until your hearts are filled with praise and the morning stars shout with you for joy.

Oh, it is Jesus. Yes, it is Jesus.
Yes, it is Jesus in my soul,
For I have touched the hem of His garment,
And His blood has made me whole.

Remember, then, that it is not the one who prays for you who is the source of your healing and strength—*it is the One to whom he or she prays.* Glory and praise and dominion and power be ascribed unto His matchless name, forever and forever, world without end. Amen and Amen.

The second mistake is mistaking *anxiety for faith*.

Anxiety is always an impediment to faith. Anticipation and hope are stepping-stones that bring you nearer to the fulfillment of your desire, but being overly anxious fastens a weight around your ankle that impedes your climb. People sometimes come rushing to meetings and demand to be prayed for immediately, and are aggravated when you ask them to wait their turn and make the spiritual preparation that is necessary. Naturally, everybody who is sick is anxious to be healed. But there's nothing in *anxiety* to heal you or to bring you relief. So many times we've seen looks of disappointment on the faces of people when there should have been signs of happiness and joy, all because they made the mistake of coming to receive their healing when they didn't know how.

Many of them are people who haven't served the Lord a day in their lives, who haven't attended a prayer meeting in years, who are too busy on Sundays to go to church, who have no thought of a real consecration of their lives to God, and who are only interested in themselves and not in the things of God. Preparation for healing is always spiritual, and you are actually nearer your healing when you believe that the healing of your soul is more important than the healing of your body. In that state, you are close to possessing the faith that will mean the end of your troubles and the beginning of a brighter and better day.

Intellectual assent is not faith. The assent of the mind might be necessary to faith, but the power of appropriation must be added to it before it can become *real faith*. Mental concentration is not faith—confessing that you believe doesn't necessarily mean that you really do. Struggling to believe with your will and mind will never bring faith, for *real faith* is a gift of God. Mountain-moving faith will never be imparted by God until your spiritual condition warrants the gift.

By this I don't mean that you must have reached a certain condition of piety, or have lived a godly life for so many days or years—the Word tells us that in the days of Jesus there were sinners who had so much faith in Him that He commended them for it. It wasn't their past that mattered, it was the fact that faith was there because their spiritual intensity at the moment of their petition was away from self, flesh, and the world and directed totally toward Jesus. I've seen men from the streets, broken and repentant at the altar, weep their way through to the Cross on which the Prince of Glory died, and receive along with their salvation a miraculous physical healing

A Slave Set Free

In one of our campaigns an unusual altar call had been given and hundreds of people had made their way to the mourners' benches to pour out their hearts to the Lord. Society people from the larger homes of the city were kneeling side by side with ill-clad inhabitants of the East Side, and mingling their prayers and tears as they sought the forgiveness of a tender and merciful Christ. When the altar call was nearly over—and small groups of people were already singing hymns of joy and salvation—an usher called our attention to a man walking down the aisle toward the altar. He was well dressed and looked prosperous, but the way his body bent forward told of a sorrow or trouble in his life.

The usher whispered to me, "I don't believe that man has been to church for twenty years. Everybody here knows him and his problem . . . poor fellow. For ten years he's been an inveterate dope addict—he's a slave to it. If that man is converted, it will shake this town."

I watched him as he slowly marched down the aisle. I could see he was struggling within himself as he halted for a brief moment at the altar. Then he went down on his knees and buried his face in his hands. Quietly I knelt at his side. He needed no helper, they would only have interfered, for his whole being was directed toward the Lord.

"Jesus . . . I am not worthy . . . I have sinned, and I come to Thee tonight, Lord, for the first time in years . . . I believe thou are the Christ . . . I believe, Lord . . . I believe. Jesus . . . Jesus. Can you save a . . . a . . . *slave?* "

He opened his eyes and looked into mine. I felt led to say, "Him that cometh unto Me I will in no wise cast out."

Five minutes passed and the great audience was on its feet singing with one accord. From the fullness of ten-thousand hearts rang the words, "Jesus breaks every fetter, and He sets me free." But down at the altar one man was still kneeling, his eyes closed, his hands clasped, his lips moving in prayer.

"I will shout hallelujah, for He sets me free," sang the audience as the rafters trembled under the volume of song and the strains floated through the open windows and out to the streets. At the altar the man was praying. He alone of these thousands was still on his knees, hands clasped, head bowed, eyes closed in prayer. "There is rest for the weary, there is rest for you," sang the congregation until it seemed that the very building itself was filled with the presence of the glory of the Lord, and our hearts would break with the joy of it all.

At the altar the man was praying over and over, "A slave, Jesus. Just a slave, Jesus . . . a slave. . . . but you promised . . . promised. Jesus . . . you promised slaves like me that you would . . ."

"On the other side of Jordan, where the tree of life is blooming, there is rest for the weary, there is rest for you," thundered the audience. Then the last echoes of the song faded away, the benediction was said, and the crowd that had seen the mighty power of the Lord that night headed for home. Outside the streetcar bells were ringing. Crowds were surging out the building doors, automobile horns were tooting, and once in awhile the strains of a hymn came floating back to the building through the open doors and windows: "Jesus breaks every fetter, and He sets me free."

Some later said they sang all the way home, on the street car, on the streets, in their cars—they couldn't seem to stop singing the praises of the Lord. But in the building there was no longer singing, just a lone man still kneeling at the altar, his eyes closed, head bowed, hands clasped, his lips moving in pleading, believing, prayer. "Only a slave, Jesus, . . . only a slave . . . but you promised, Jesus . . . that you would save . . . unto the uttermost . . ."

Then down the aisle there came the Living Word of God, the One Whom the angel Gabriel said should be called Jesus, "for He shall save His people from their sins." Down the aisle He came, the Man of Sorrows, who knew, who understood, who loved and who cared. No eye could see Him, no ear could catch the tread of His feet. But He stopped at the heart cry of a penitent sinner, just as He stopped at the cry of blind Bartimaeus on the Jericho highway, and listened to the man praying, "Just a slave, Jesus, helpless . . . weak . . . help me, please."

A moment later in a city far beyond the stars, where the streets are paved with gold and the walls are of jasper, the bells were pealing and the angel choirs were singing, for a soul—a slave to dope and sin—had been redeemed and set free, and heaven was filled with joy.

At the altar the man stood with his arms lifted toward heaven—his eyes were open and lit with the radiance of heaven's own joy, and his face was aglow with a glory that was divine. He was shouting with joy, "A slave, Lord Jesus, and you rescued me . . . a slave, and now I am free, Jesus! Oh, Jesus . . . glory . . . glory . . . glory, Lord." Through the open windows we could still hear many singing as they drove out of the parking lot, "Jesus breaks every fetter, and He sets me free."

Healed of the dope habit. Chains broken, shackles smashed, barriers torn away, saved and healed by power divine.

It's later in the week. A man is standing at the altar of a large church listening to the words of the preacher: "I give you then the right hand of fellowship and welcome you into the communion of this church. May God richly bless you, my brother . . . and make this church a blessing to you." The congregation breathes a fervent "Amen." The man turns from the altar; head erect; eyes tear-dimmed but filled with happiness and joy; he *used* to be a slave . . . just a slave . . . until he met Jesus. *Jesus, Savior, healer, breaks every fetter . . . and He sets me free.*

So we find in coming for our healing that it is not because of our righteousness or our church membership, or our deeds of Christian charity and love, that we can lay claim to the promise of the Lord, but it is because at that moment we give ourselves unreservedly to Him—to His promise and to His Word and take our healing from Him in simple faith. A broken spirit and a contrite heart and a feeling of unworthiness is generally an assurance of faith enough for healing, while on the other hand many people lose the blessing because they feel they are entitled to it.

Passive and Active Faith

Your attitude when coming to the Lord for the healing of your body should be one of a faith in which all the elements of doubt have been eliminated. It's the same kind of attitude that you should have when you have finished the prayer of supplication and have started the prayer of praise. When a man supplicates, it proves that he does not possess the thing for which he asks. When a man follows the supplication prayer by the utterance of praise it proves that he "believes that he receives" (or "has received") the thing for which he asks. It seems to me that a feeling of anticipation and joy would be noticeable on the face of the person who knew with believing faith—and that is the kind you must have—that their cancer or rheumatism was to melt away in a few moments under the touch of the Lord. It's good to ask, it's blessed to petition, but the benediction falls when you receive. There are two kinds of faith: *passive* and *active*. Passive faith says, "I believe Jesus can heal me; I believe Jesus has healed others; the work is possible; I believe that with all my heart." Active faith says, "I believe Jesus can heal, and praise the Lord I am *now* healed. The promise is mine. I take it and I *now* possess it!"

A Little Child Shall Lead Them

A little girl is on the platform, standing before the pulpit, eager and anxious for the prayer of faith. It's evident that she has been crying, but the tears have been wiped away and a smile lights her face.

"How old are you, little sweetheart?" I asked.

"I'm seven, sir," she replied.

"Do you love Jesus? I'm sure you must, for you know Jesus loves little children. Tell me dear, what is your trouble?"

Her answer is a pained expression as she slowly lifts her limb and shows a badly handicapped and deformed foot encased in a special large and bulky shoe. Under one arm, however, she's holding something that she seems to value. It's wrapped in a piece of newspaper, and it seems peculiar that she should be carrying such a package up to the platform.

"What have you in the parcel little girl?" I asked her.

Her answer was a change from her expression of pain to a sweet smile. Slowly, in full view of the audience, she unfastened the string and unrolled the paper and to our astonished eyes she presented a new . . . *shoe*. She held it proudly, and then quietly exclaimed, "I brought it with me so I could wear it home."

Faith! Faith! Faith! Here was faith unsullied, unspoiled, untarnished by the ravages of a so-called rationalism that is nothing more nor less than gross unbelief masquerading as higher criticism. Here in this little girl was the faith that Jesus talked about as she reached out and stood upon the promises. Sweet, simple, childlike faith—her Master had spoken and she believed. "Except ye become converted and become as little children ye cannot enter the kingdom of heaven." I took that shoe and looked at it, and then turned back to the little girl. Her hands, now freed, were being slowly raised to heaven and her little lips were moving in prayer. I placed upon her forehead the oil of anointing and prayed to the friend of little children, and then said as I finished, "My little sister, receive your healing in the name of Jesus."

No expression of ecstatic joy left her lips. No shout of glory, no word of praise. No exuberance of feeling, no outburst of emotionalism—she just looked at those on the platform and smiled. "God bless you, little sweetheart," I said, as handed her back her shoe. She took it and very deliberately walked over to a vacant chair and, stooping over, began to unfasten the shoe on the deformed foot. People watched her in amazement. Once she looked up and smiled. Then with a quick jerk off came the old shoe and, as she placed it by the side of the chair, she said, "I won't need that any more, will I?"

She never put that old shoe back on again. When she walked off the stage it was with her new shoe on the foot that had been deformed.

"Who healed you, dear?" someone asked.

"Jesus," she replied without hesitating.

She walked to the end of the platform, stopped a moment and then went on again, saying loudly as she went, "Somebody throw that old shoe away; I won't want it anymore."

Out in the audience the people were sobbing. Strong men who came to criticize stayed to pray. Women whose lives had been centered in themselves, waited to kneel at the feet of the friendless prisoner of Pilate's judgment hall and tell Him they would serve and love Him the rest of their lives.

The little child who led them to prayer and adoration had taught a great audience the difference between passive and active faith.

4

How to Keep Your Healing

This question is often asked: "Is it possible to lose your healing after once the touch of a loving Savior's hand has been laid upon your head, or the divine voice has spoken to you telling you that you are made whole?"

To this question there is but one answer: *yes*. It is possible for you to lose your healing and to sink back again into the state that you were in, spiritually or physically, before the Lord by His grace healed you.

In the fifth chapter of the Gospel according to Saint John, there is the story of a man who was healed by Jesus at the pool called Bethesda. In the story we're told that there was a feast of the Jews held in the city of Jerusalem. In all probability this was the Feast of the Passover, and Jesus had gone to the city to be with His disciples and, undoubtedly, to minister to the waiting multitudes.

Close by the sheep market was a pool whose waters were troubled at certain periods by the touch of an angel. Around the edge of the pool a waiting multitude of sick and impotent folk were always gathered, waiting for the angel's touch.

It seems significant that this pool, called Bethesda, which means a place of mercy, was near the busy mart of human industry, the sheep market, and that Jesus was found in the place where He was needed. Whether in the busy marts of human industry, or in stately cathedrals , or village chapels, or among a great congregation of people, Jesus Christ is found wherever there is the cry of a hungry heart, wherever there is a sob of distress, wherever there is the need for the touch of a Savior's hand. *It is in the midst of need that we always find Jesus.*

And so it was that Jesus passed by the pool that was the place of mercy, and saw there an impotent man who had an infirmity thirty and eight years.

In tenderest love and compassion the eyes of the Master were focused upon him, and Jesus seemed to see through the rough exterior down to the very intent of his heart. He knew that man's need just as He knows yours. He knew that this man who had been suffering for thirty-eight years could not find help in any power but the one that He possessed. Because Jesus saw the need, and knew that He had power to meet that need, He said to the man, "Wilt thou be made whole?" (John 5:6).

Oh friends, weary and sin sick, heavily laden with the cares and tolls of a weary world, Jesus would say the same to you, "Wilt thou be made whole?"

Oh brothers and sisters of mine, suffering the pains of disease and knowing the gnawing of corruption in those bodies of yours, don't you hear, too, the voice of the Nazarene, "Wilt thou be made whole?"

And you who are so busy and distressed with the cares of the home and the children, looking and longing through the darkness of your night for the dawning of a happy day, "Wilt thou be made whole?"

And you, too, little children, with your voices hushed because of the sickness and pain in your little bodies, "Wilt thou be made whole?"

Jesus, tender, loving, sympathetic Man of Galilee, is standing by your side and, looking into your eyes, is asking you directly this one question, *"Wilt thou be made whole?"*

The impotent man gazed into the face of Jesus, and not understanding at first the intent of His question, said to Him, "Sir, I have no man, when the water is troubled, to put me into the pool; but while I am coming, another steppeth down before me" (John 5:7). (We don't always understand the intent of Jesus' questions. We don't always grasp the meaning of His Word. We don't always know the depth of divine truth that's contained in the precious Book—the Word of God. But we do know that regardless of our weaknesses, misunderstandings, and lack of knowledge, Jesus is *always* willing to help.)

Jesus saith unto him, "Rise, take up thy bed and walk."

I would that every sinner and every saint could know that Jesus came to break every fetter and to set every prisoner free! If we have faith in Him, the Lion of the Tribe of Judah will break every chain and give us the victory—glorious, wonderful, eternal victory—again and again! Jesus came to give you sunshine for your shadow, the oil of joy for mourning, and beauty for ashes—not just in the hereafter, but in the here and now.

The Prodigal Son

Some time ago in a land across the sea an evangelist was conducting a revival meeting, and the power of God had descended and numbers of people were finding Christ as a personal Savior. On a memorable Saturday night the evangelist was to preach on the story of the Prodigal Son, and requested a certain soprano singer in his choir to sing the old hymn, "Where Is My Wandering Boy Tonight?"

The singer looked into the eyes of the evangelist and said, "Sir, I can't sing that hymn! Any hymn will do but that. I would love to sing it, but I'm afraid it's impossible."

"Why have you an aversion to that particular hymn?" he asked.

For a moment she looked as if she were about to cry, then she said, "Fourteen years ago my husband died, and my only boy, who was then fourteen and had a delivery job, thought that he should keep all the money he earned and not help with our household expenses. One day when I tried to talk to him about it, he burst into a fit of temper and left the house. From that day to this I haven't seen him."

Tears ran down her cheeks as she continued, "Oh, sir, is it any wonder when the strains of that hymn come to my ears that my heart is almost broken? I couldn't sing, sir, I would surely break down before I finished and ruin the song."

"But, madam," said the evangelist, "I want you to sing that hymn because that's my subject tonight. Who knows, perhaps the Master will bless it to the salvation of some soul, for you'll sing it from a heart filled with feeling and love."

That night the Church was crowded to overflowing. The evangelist went to the pulpit, gave out his Bible text, and told the story of how the father welcomed home his prodigal son. At the conclusion of the sermon, just before the altar call, the singer rose to her feet and sang with a clear, ringing, voice:

> Where is my wand'ring boy tonight,
> The boy of my tenderest care.
> The boy that was once my joy and light,
> The boy of his mother's prayer."

She struggled bravely through that verse, but in the chorus she broke down, then composed herself and picked up the refrain and carried to the end. By the time she reached the second verse her body was shaking with sobs, but she managed to struggle through:

> Once he was pure as morning dew,
> As he played at his mother's knee;
> No face was so bright, no heart more true,
> And none was as happy as he.

Again she sang through the chorus with streaming eyes until at last the climax of her emotions and prayer was reached in the words:

> Go for my wand'ring boy tonight;
> Go search for him where you will;
> But bring him to me with all his blight,
> And tell him I love him still.

From the back of the building a young man, clothed in rags and tatters, rose to his feet. Slowly he made his way down the center aisle of the building. When he reached the front of the church he went the end of the altar where there were steps leading up the platform to where the woman was singing. There he fell on his knees in front of her and, with a voice that could be heard throughout the building, cried, "Mother, do you mean it—do you mean it, Mother?

The woman looked down into the face of her long-lost son, and her cry of gratitude ascended to God. Raising him to his feet she led him to the altar rail, and there together they told the sinner's Friend about a contrite and repentant heart— and that night salvation came into the soul of the son for whom she had prayed so long.

Did she mean it? Were the words of her song true? Ah, yes, my friend! You who have known the power of a mother's love, know that in spite of his deserting her and his sins, his mother loved him still. Let me say here that if you know the love of Christ, you know also that in spite of the blight of sin He loves you still.

The one burning message that I would like to bring into your heart, the story that I would like to inscribe indelibly upon the tablet of your mind, is the story that Jesus loves you. In spite of the scars, in spite of the wounds, in spite of your sins, Jesus loves you. It should bring hope to your heart and encouragement to your soul to know that regardless of your condition you have a lover in Jesus Christ. In Him you have a High Priest who sympathizes with you, understands you, knows all about you, and who loves you with a love that was so deep and strong that it sent Him to the Cross in your place.

The Pool of Bethesda

You're by the side of the pool called Bethesda. You're by the "Waters of Mercy" waiting for the touch of an angel hand and the stirring of the pool. But as you wait let me remind you that Jesus is looking into your eyes and saying, as He did to the impotent man and to blind Bartimaeus, "What wilt thou that I should do unto thee?"

Then as you gaze into His eyes, and faith takes hold of your heart and doubts vanish like the night before the dawning of the day, comes the promise of the Lord, "My grace is sufficient for thee; rise, take up thy bed and walk. In my strength shalt thou go out to walk in newness of life."

And so it was that healing came to the impotent man at the Pool. There was a group of people in that day, just as there is today, who are ever ready to criticize, and they immediately started to destroy the faith of the man who was made whole, and tried to undermine the foundation of faith upon which he had placed his feet.

It's easy to find fault, and anybody can criticize, but I've never been able to understand the fault finding and criticism that is sometimes offered in the face of a work that is self-evident. When people are healed, and you can see that they're healed and are standing before you, it's inconceivable to believe that sometimes people will say they doubt divine healing and believe that Jesus only healed in the days when He walked the earth.

If a thing is self-evident, it must be a fact. The thing we can see with our eyes is the thing that we must believe. Jesus always brings sufficient proof to any inquiring heart as to the truthfulness of His statements and the integrity of His Word, if only we ask and seek and knock.

In the days of Jesus, people criticized because the healing occurred on the Sabbath day. In these days, people criticize because healings occur on *any* day, even though the healings are just as evident as the healing of the man at the pool of Bethesda.

The Healer is the same. His love and truth and power is the same. And why should not Jesus of Nazareth walk the streets of your city with the same love and compassion in His heart as when He walked the hills of Judea and the streets of Jerusalem?

There's a verse that I want to draw your attention to that contains a thought that should burn itself into the soul of every man and woman who goes to Jesus for healing. That's a statement contained in John 5:14 when Jesus found the healed man in the temple and said to him, "Behold, thou art made whole; sin no more, lest a worse thing come unto thee."

In this passage we find the truth that inasmuch as we can obtain healing, we can also lose it. I believe that if we go back into the realms of sin, if we deviate from the paths of righteousness, we can lose our healing and perhaps the last condition of our bodies will be worse than the first.

As "we walk in the light, as He is in the light, we have fellowship one with another, and the blood of Jesus Christ his Son cleanseth us from all sin" (1 John 1:7). So long as we walk in the light of truth, and fasten all our hopes upon Jesus, and keep our affections centered around the old rugged Cross, and maintain an active faith in God's promise and Word, we will keep our healing.

I could write many stories of people who have lost their healing who could have maintained it. It's true that in comparison to the number that keep their healing they are very few. But oh, I would warn against going back to the flesh pots of Egypt and to the sins of the old life, when before you are the promised hills and vales, the mountains and glades, and the rivers that flow with milk and honey.

The man at the pool of Bethesda told everybody he met that it was Jesus who healed him, and by the word of his testimony he made the praises of the Galilean ring far and wide. We are told in the Scriptures that we overcome by the blood of the Lamb and the word of our testimony. It seems to me to be a mark of ingratitude for people never to tell the story of the Great Physician when they have experienced healing, or never to tell of the glory of the Savior when they have known what it is to be saved.

It seems to me that sometimes the very stones would cry out the glory of the Lord when our hearts are closed and our lips are silent, and we take God's benefits and blessings in a matter-of-fact way. We need the spirit of the Psalmist who, with his heart bursting with a radiance of heavenly joy exclaimed, "they cry unto the LORD in their trouble, and he saveth them out of their distresses. He sent his word, and healed them, and delivered them from their destructions. Oh that men would praise the LORD for his goodness, and for his wonderful works to the children of men!"

Testimony is a messenger of God to hearts that today might be like yours once was. Testimony is a key that will open the door for aching, weary feet to see a path that will lead to a better day. Testimony is a herald that will proclaim the story of a Cross to a world that is heavily laden and worn. Testimony may be the road that will lead to the healing of a weary, pain-racked body and a life that is filled with the darkness of suffering and sickness.

Ah, my friend, you remember the lepers—only one returned to give thanks unto the Lord. "Were there not ten cleansed? But where are the nine?" When you go to a church altar, or kneel in your home to pray for the touch of the Master's hand, look up to Him and in believing faith *receive*. Then radiant with the joy of salvation, happy in the experience of a healed body, go out to let your light shine before men and to tell the story of a Christ who died to save you.

You say your affliction is a cross? Bear it then; and under the Master's guidance the cross of wood will turn to a crown of gold and the burden will change to a ministry of joy.

> I will cherish the old rugged Cross,
> Till my trophies at last I lay down;
> I will cling to the old, rugged Cross,
> And exchange it some day for a crown.